Jack C. Richards & Chuck Sandy

Passages

Third Edition

T0343932

Student's Book
with eBook

2 B

CAMBRIDGE
UNIVERSITY PRESS

CAMBRIDGE
UNIVERSITY PRESS

University Printing House, Cambridge CB2 8BS, United Kingdom

One Liberty Plaza, 20th Floor, New York, NY 10006, USA

477 Williamstown Road, Port Melbourne, VIC 3207, Australia

314–321, 3rd Floor, Plot 3, Splendor Forum, Jasola District Centre, New Delhi – 110025, India

103 Penang Road, #05-06/07, Visioncrest Commercial, Singapore 238467

Cambridge University Press is part of the University of Cambridge.

It furthers the University's mission by disseminating knowledge in the pursuit of education, learning and research at the highest international levels of excellence.

www.cambridge.org
Information on this title: www.cambridge.org/9781009040853

First published 1998
Second edition 2008
Reprinted 2019
Third edition 2015
Update to Third edition published 2021

20 19 18 17 16 15 14 13 12 11 10 9 8 7 6 5 4 3 2

Printed in Poland by Opolgraf

A catalogue record for this publication is available from the British Library

ISBN 978-1-009-04083-9 Student's Book 2 with eBook
ISBN 978-1-009-04084-6 Student's Book 2A with eBook
ISBN 978-1-009-04085-3 Student's Book 2B with eBook
ISBN 978-1-009-04092-1 Student's Book 2 with Digital Pack
ISBN 978-1-009-04093-8 Student's Book 2A with Digital Pack
ISBN 978-1-009-04094-5 Student's Book 2B with Digital Pack
ISBN 978-1-107-62726-0 Workbook 2
ISBN 978-1-107-62734-5 Workbook 2A
ISBN 978-1-107-62780-2 Workbook 2B
ISBN 978-1-107-62766-6 Teacher's Edition 2 with Assessment Audio
ISBN 978-1-107-62749-9 Class Audio 2
ISBN 978-1-009-04095-2 Full Contact 2 with Digital Pack
ISBN 978-1-009-04096-9 Full Contact 2A with Digital Pack
ISBN 978-1-009-04097-6 Full Contact 2B with Digital Pack
ISBN 978-1-107-62764-2 DVD 2
ISBN 978-1-107-68650-2 Presentation Plus 2

Additional resources for this publication at cambridgeone.org

Cambridge University Press has no responsibility for the persistence or accuracy of URLs for external or third-party internet websites referred to in this publication, and does not guarantee that any content on such websites is, or will remain, accurate or appropriate. Information regarding prices, travel timetables, and other factual information given in this work is correct at the time of first printing but Cambridge University Press does not guarantee the accuracy of such information thereafter.

Art direction, book design, layout services, and photo research: Q2A / Bill Smith
Audio production: John Marshall Media
Video production: Steadman Productions

Authors' Acknowledgments

A great number of people contributed to the development of *Passages Third Edition*. Particular thanks are owed to the following reviewers and institutions, as their insights and suggestions have helped define the content and format of the third edition:

Paulo A. Machado, Rio de Janeiro, Brazil; Simone C. Wanguestel, Niterói, Brazil; Athiná Arcadinos Leite, **ACBEU**, Salvador, Brazil; Lauren Osowski, **Adult Learning Center**, Nashua, NH, USA; Brenda Victoria, **AIF System**, Santiago, Dominican Republic; Alicia Mitchell-Boncquet, **ALPS Language School**, Seattle, WA, USA; Scott C. Welsh, **Arizona State University**, Tempe, AZ, USA; Silvia Corrêa, **Associação Alumni**, São Paulo, Brazil; Henrick Oprea, **Atlantic Idiomas**, Brasília, Brazil; Márcia Lima, **B.A. English School**, Goiânia, Brazil; Carlos Andrés Mejía Gómez, **BNC Centro Colombo Americano Pereira**, Pereira, Colombia; Tanja Jakimoska, **Brava Training**, Rio de Janeiro, Brazil; Paulo Henrique Gomes de Abreu, **Britannia International English**, Rio de Janeiro, Brazil; Gema Kuri Rodríguez, **Business & English**, Puebla, Mexico; Isabela Villas Boas, **Casa Thomas Jefferson**, Brasília, Brazil; Inara Lúcia Castillo Couto, **CEL-LEP**, São Paulo, Brazil; Ana Cristina Hebling Meira, **Centro Cultural Brasil-Estados Unidos**, Campinas, Brazil; Juliana Costa da Silva, **Centro de Cultura Anglo Americana**, Rio de Janeiro, Brazil; Heriberto Díaz Vázquez, **Centro de Investigación y Docencia Económicas**, Mexico City, Mexico; D. L. Dorantes-Salas, **Centro de Investigaciones Biológicas del Noroeste**, La Paz, Mexico; Elizabeth Carolina Llatas Castillo, **Centro Peruano Americano El Cultural**, Trujillo-La Libertad, Peru; Márcia M. A. de Brito, **Chance Language Center**, Rio de Janeiro, Brazil; Rosalinda Heredia, **Colegio Motolinia**, San Juan del Río, Mexico; Maria Regina Pereira Filgueiras, **College Language Center**, Londrina, Brazil; Lino Mendoza Rodriguez, **Compummunicate**, Izúcar de Matamoros, Mexico; Maria Lucia Sciamarelli, **Cultura Inglesa**, Campinas, Brazil; Elisabete Thess, **Cultura Inglesa**, Petrópolis, Brazil; Catarina M. B. Pontes Kruppa, **Cultura Inglesa**, São Paulo, Brazil; Sheila Lima, **Curso Oxford**, Rio de Janeiro, Brazil; Elaine Florencio, Beth Vasconcelos, **English House Corporate**, Rio de Janeiro, Brazil; Vasti Rodrigues e Silva, **Fox Idiomas**, Rio de Janeiro, Brazil; Ricardo Ramos Miguel Cézar, Walter Júnior Ribeiro Silva, **Friends Language Center**, Itapaci, Brazil; Márcia Maria Pedrosa Sá Freire de Souza, **IBEU**, Rio de Janeiro, Brazil; Jerusa Rafael, **IBEUV**, Vitória, Brazil; Lilianne de Souza Oliveira, **ICBEU**, Manaus, Brazil; Liviane Santana Paulino de Carvalho, **ICBEU**, São Luís, Brazil; Manuel Marrufo Vásquez, **iempac Instituto de Enseñanza del Idioma Ingles**, Tequila, Mexico; Nora Aquino, **Instituto de Ciencias y Humanidades Tabasco**, Villahermosa, Mexico; Andrea Grimaldo, **Instituto Laurens**, Monterrey, Mexico; Cenk Aykut, Staci Jenkins, Kristen Okada, **Interactive College of Technology**, Chamblee, GA, USA; Imeen Manahan-Vasquez, Zuania Serrano, **Interactive Learning Systems**, Pasadena, TX, USA; Nicholas J. Jackson, **Jackson English School**, Uruapan, Mexico; Marc L. Cummings, **Jefferson Community and Technical College**, Louisville, KY, USA; Solange Nery Veloso, **Nery e Filho Idiomas**, Rio de Janeiro, Brazil; Tomas Sparano Martins, **Phil Young's English School**, Curitiba, Brazil; Paulo Cezar Lira Torres, **PRIME Language Center**, Vitória, Brazil; Angie Vasconcellos, **Robin English School**, Petrópolis, Brazil; Barbara Raifsnider, **San Diego Community College District**, San Diego, CA, USA; James Drury de Matos Fonseca, **SENAC**, Fortaleza, Brazil; Manoel Fialho da Silva Neto, **SENAC**, Recife, Brazil; Marilyn Ponder, **Tecnológico de Monterrey**, Irapuato, Mexico; Linda M. Holden, **The College of Lake County**, Grayslake, IL, USA; Janaína da Silva Cardoso, **UERJ**, Rio de Janeiro, Brazil; Gustavo Reges Ferreira, Sandlei Moraes de Oliveira, **UFES**, Vitória, Brazil; Nancy Alarcón Mendoza, **UNAM, Facultad de Estudios Superiores Zaragoza**, Mexico City, Mexico; Rosa Awilda López Fernández, **UNAPEC**, Santo Domingo, Dominican Republic; Vera Lúcia Ratide, **Unilínguas**, São Leopoldo, Brazil; Elsa Yolanda Cruz Maldonado, **Universidad Autónoma de Chiapas**, Tapachula, Mexico; Deida Perea, **Universidad Autónoma de Ciudad Juárez**, Ciudad Juárez, Mexico; Gabriela Ladrón de Guevara de León, **Universidad Autónoma de la Ciudad de México**, Mexico City, Mexico; Juan Manuel Ardila Prada, **Universidad Autónoma de Occidente**, Cali, Colombia; Lizzete G. Acosta Cruz, **Universidad Autónoma de Zacatecas**, Fresnillo, Mexico; Ary Guel, Fausto Noriega, Areli Martínez Suaste, **Universidad Autónoma de Zacatecas**, Zacatecas, Mexico; Gabriela Cortés Sánchez, **Universidad Autónoma Metropolitana Azcapotzalco**, Mexico City, Mexico; Secundino Isabeles Flores, Guillermo Guadalupe Duran Garcia, Maria Magdalena Cass Zubiria, **Universidad de Colima**, Colima, Mexico; Alejandro Rodríguez Sánchez, **Universidad del Golfo de México Norte**, Orizaba, Mexico; Fabiola Meneses Argüello, **Universidad La Salle Cancún**, Cancún, Mexico; Claudia Isabel Fierro Castillo, **Universidad Politécnica de Chiapas**, Tuxtla Gutierrez, Mexico; Eduardo Aguirre Rodríguez, M.A. Carolina Labastida Villa, **Universidad Politécnica de Quintana Roo**, Cancún, Mexico; Gabriela de Jesús Aubry González, **Universidad TecMilenio Campus Veracruz**, Boca del Rio, Mexico; Frank Ramírez Marín, **Universidad Veracruzana**, Boca del Río, Mexico.

Additional thanks are owed to Alex Tilbury for revising the Self-assessment charts, Paul MacIntyre for revising the Grammar Plus section, and Karen Kawaguchi for writing the Vocabulary Plus section.

Welcome to **Passages!**

Congratulations! You have learned the basics; now it's time to raise your English to a whole new level.

Your journey through each unit of *Passages Third Edition* will include a range of activities that will **progressively expand your language ability** in a variety of contexts, including formal and informal communication.

Along the way, you will encounter frequent communication reviews and progress checks that will **systematically consolidate your learning**, while **additional grammar and vocabulary practice** is available whenever you need it in the Grammar Plus and Vocabulary Plus sections in the back of this book.

RAISING YOUR ENGLISH TO A WHOLE NEW LEVEL
Unique features to boost your English proficiency!

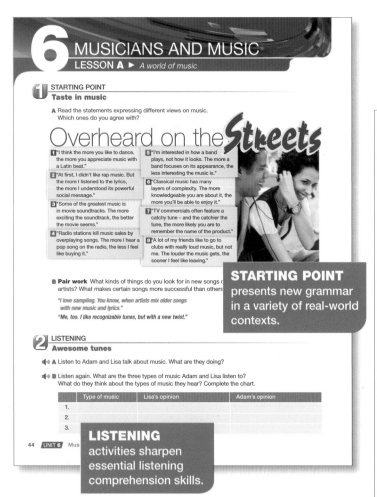

STARTING POINT presents new grammar in a variety of real-world contexts.

LISTENING activities sharpen essential listening comprehension skills.

GRAMMAR is explored in context and builds on previously encountered structures.
Grammar Plus: extra grammar explanations and practice when you need it!

4 VOCABULARY & SPEAKING
Different attitudes

A Look at these expressions. Which ones express a positive attit__ attitude, or a neutral attitude? Write +, –, or ~.

____ 1. aware of
____ 2. curious about
____ 3. sick of
____ 4. fed up with
____ 5. familiar with
____ 6. suspicious of
____ 7 intimidated by
____ 8. knowledgeable abou__

B Group work Look at the list of inventions and technologies. __
What are your feelings about them? Discuss with your group.

1. spacecraft for private flights
2. touch-screen technology
3. speech-translation technology
4. video surveillance
5. wearable electronics
6. mobile apps
7. laser surgery
8. robots

"So, what do you think about spacecraft for private flights?"
"I'm a little intimidated by the idea of being in space. I'm curious about it, but I wouldn't try it."

VOCABULARY PLUS *see page 132*

VOCABULARY
expands upon prior knowledge and improves vocabulary building skills.
NEW *Vocabulary Plus:*
extra vocabulary practice when you need it!

5 DISCUSSION
Tech savvy?

A Are you a technophile or a technophobe? Complete the survey to find out.

TECHNOPHILE or TECHNOPHOBE?

	Agree (2 pts.)	Not Sure (1 pt.)	Disagree (0 pts.)
1. If technology permits it, I would favor the development of machines that surpass humans in intelligence.			
2. Governments need to generously fund research and development in technology.			
3. Everyone should try to stay informed about the latest innovations in technology.			
4. Genetic technologies should be used to gradually improv__ the human body over the course of generations.			
5. Science and technology will someday solve the world's problems of famine, war, disease, and overcrowding.			
6. It's important to acquire new technological devices short__ after they come out.			
7. Social media has a positive effect on people's social live__			
8. Being connected to the Internet is a human right.			

SCORE **0–4** You are a technophobe, a person who has a strong mistrust of technology.
5–8 While not in love with technology, you see the need for it in our world.

B Group work Discuss your answers to the survey. Ta__
your choices and whether or not you agree with your __

SPEAKING
activities spark lively discussions focusing on interesting and relevant situations.

24

Passages Third Edition is a two-level course that will open the door to communicating with greater fluency and proficiency, with:

- **more sophisticated** real-world grammar and vocabulary,
- **thought-provoking** discussions and academic writing activities,
- **more challenging** listening and reading comprehension topics.

6 WRITING
Compare-and-contrast essays

A compare-and-contrast essay presents the similarities and differences of two or more things. The thesis statement expresses your position on the subject, and it is followed by supporting paragraphs that discuss similarities and differences.

A Read the essay and circle the thesis statement. Then match each paragraph to __
the headings below. Underline the words that show __

____ introduction   ____ differences   ____ con__

THE BEATLES

1 Although the Beatles and the Rolling Stones have both been called the "greatest rock 'n' roll band of all time," the prize should go to the Rolling Stones. While both bands have had a huge influence on popular music, the Beatles broke up in 1970, and the Rolling Stones went on recording and performing for over 50 years.

2 Both the Beatles and the Rolling Stones began as four-member British bands that first became popular in the 1960s. The two bands released their first records within a year of each other, and both featured a pair of talented songwriters: Paul McCartney and John Lennon for the Beatles, and Mick Jagger and Keith Richards for the Rolling Stones. Like the Rolling Stones, the Beatles were famous for their cutting-edge style at the time of their debut, and both bands were known for their energetic stage performances.

B Choose two bands, singers, or musical styles to c__
make a list of similarities and differences. Then con__
that expresses your view.

C Write a four-paragraph essay. Make sure it has an __
thesis statement, two paragraphs describing simila__
an effective conclusion.

D Pair work Take turns reading your essays. Do no__
Can your partner guess your point of view?

WRITING
tasks build academic writing skills through step-by-step activities.

6 READING
Technology and friendship

A Pair work Discuss these questions. Then read the article to compare your ideas with the author's.

1. What are some ways that interacting online might encourage people to connect in real life?
2. How could social media help shy students participate more in class?

READING
passages drawn from authentic sources promote critical thinking and analysis.

HOW SOCIAL MEDIA "FRIENDS" TRANSLATE INTO REAL-LIFE FRIENDSHIPS

When social media first gained attention, I heard many people say online connections couldn't possibly be real friends. Some even feared people might trade face-to-face interaction for a virtual life online. But now the majority of the people I know consider at least some of their online friends to be like extended family. Which made me wonder – does social media actually encourage people to connect "in real life"?

One example of online life translating into real-life interaction happens on *Mashable*'s Social Media Day, when thousands of people attend in-person meet-ups to celebrate the power of online connections. Another example is location-based apps that help users connect face-to-face by allowing them to see who else has checked in at the same store, restaurant, or party – or even who is living in a city they plan to visit. They might then decide to seek each other out "in real life."

A Pew Internet and American Life Project report found that people using social networking sites have more close relationships and receive more support than others. They are also more likely to reconnect with old friends and use social networking to keep up with those they are already close to.

Other research shows that social media may also deepen what could otherwise be passing relationships. A study by Dr. Rey Junco found that college students who interacted with each other and their professors on Twitter were more likely to meet outside class to study. They also developed

unexpected real-life connections and were also more likely to ask questions in class.

"What I find most fascinating is that I've consistently seen that students who start a course being more introverted and not speaking up during class discussions become more extroverted and participate more when encouraged to communicate through social media with their professors and their classmates," Junco said.

However, if social media does increase the likelihood of real-life interaction, it can also sometimes complicate it. When fans of social media meet face-to-face, their computers and mobile devices may actually make the meeting less productive. Instead of looking at each other, they may be glued to their screens!

Source: "How Social Media 'Friends' Translate Into Real-Life Friendships," by Terri Thornton, Mediashift

B Group work Discuss these questions. Then share your answers with the class.

1. In what ways are virtual friendships similar to and different from real-life friendships?
2. Would you be more or less willing to share ideas on social media than you would in class? Why?
3. What other issues and complications might come up when online friends meet face-to-face?

LESSON B Make new friends, but keep the old . . .   **9**

KEEP MOVING UP!
More support is always available – when and where you need it!

The **WORKBOOK** provides extensive practice of grammar and vocabulary as well as additional reading and writing activities.

The **DIGITAL WORKBOOK** – a digital version of the Workbook – enables your teacher to provide instant feedback on your work.

AUDIO AND VIDEO on Cambridge One allows students to review on their own.

cambridgeone.org

v

Plan of **BOOK 2B**

SPEAKING	LISTENING	WRITING	READING
■ Discussing trends ■ Talking about personal changes ■ Talking about the results of a survey on coping with change	■ A corporate executive speaks about the attitudes of different generations in the workplace ■ Two people talk about a volunteer program	■ Writing about a personal experience ■ Providing background information and giving details	■ "Leaving the Rat Race for the Simple Life": Reflections on a major change in lifestyle
■ Talking about the best ways to shop for different items ■ Discussing compulsive shopping ■ Discussing the ethics of undercover marketing strategies	■ Two people talk about their shopping preferences ■ Three radio advertisements	■ Supporting an opinion ■ Writing a composition using details and examples to support an opinion about shopping	■ "Word-of-Mouth Marketing": Testing the power of word-of-mouth as a marketing strategy
■ Discussing the ethics of using animals in different fields ■ Discussing a survey on ethics associated with animals ■ Discussing ways of being in touch with nature	■ News reports on animals that help people ■ The manager of an eco-resort describes its features to a reporter	■ Organizing information into clear categories ■ Writing a classification essay	■ "A Summer Job that's a Walk in the Park": The daily tasks of a park ranger fellow in New York City
■ Discussing the qualities of effective communicators ■ Discussing a survey on public speaking ■ Discussing opinions about language issues ■ Talking about "text speak" and its appropriateness ■ Role-playing different ways of speaking	■ An expert gives advice on how to make effective presentations ■ Three one-sided conversations	■ Persuasive writing ■ Supporting a position ■ Arguing against the opposing position	■ "Slang Abroad": Different varieties of English
■ Discussing people who have had an impact on the world ■ Discussing the qualities and values of exceptional people ■ Discussing quotations from high achievers ■ Talking about heroic behavior in everyday life	■ A motivational speaker talks about the qualities of high achievers ■ Two people talk about others who have made a difference in their lives	■ Organizing information in chronological order ■ Writing a biographical profile	■ "Ann Cotton, Social Entrepreneur": Advice from a successful NGO executive
■ Discussing successful companies ■ Discussing job advertisements ■ Discussing a survey on ideal working conditions ■ Analyzing the qualities of the ideal job ■ Discussing the qualities of a successful worker	■ Two people discuss unsuccessful business ventures ■ Three people talk about workshops they attended	■ Understanding the parts of a formal letter ■ Writing a formal letter	■ "The Value of Difference": Individual differences in the workplace

7 CHANGING TIMES

LESSON A ▶ *Lifestyles in transition*

1 STARTING POINT
How we are changing

A People's lifestyles are changing more quickly than ever before. Have you noticed any of these trends in your community?

Lifestyle Trends

1 Social exercise programs that offer fun group workouts are on the rise. Enrollment in cycling, strength-training, dance, and yoga classes has never been higher.

2 Hybrid cars, powered by both gas and electricity, are an option that more people are choosing in order to save money and reduce pollution.

3 More professionals whose managers allow it are opting to telecommute, or work from home.

4 More and more shoppers are looking for recyclable products that companies can manufacture sustainably.

5 Children are learning foreign languages at earlier ages than ever before. Some elementary schools now offer classes for children whom they once considered too young.

6 A growing number of people who are concerned with the effects of pesticides on the environment are buying organic produce.

7 These days, people who are not happy with their bodies are more likely to resort to cosmetic surgery.

8 Tourists whose destinations are foreign countries are taking more trips, traveling greater distances, and spending more money.

B **Pair work** Discuss the good points and bad points of each trend. Which trends do you think are the most beneficial?

"Social exercise programs are great because they encourage more people to get fit."

"I think many people get a better workout by themselves. They exercise more and socialize less!"

2 DISCUSSION
Current trends

A **Pair work** Think of a current trend in your country, community, or among people you know for as many of these areas as you can.

- education / schools
- nature / environment
- shopping / stores
- food / restaurants
- health / fitness
- travel / tourism
- science / technology
- appearance / fashion

B **Group work** Join another pair. Share your ideas and choose the three most significant trends. Then prepare a short presentation for the class explaining the trends and why you think they are the most important.

"One trend we discussed is that a lot of people are into ecotourism lately. This is certainly an important and beneficial trend because . . . "

GRAMMAR

Optional and required relative pronouns

In defining relative clauses, when the relative pronoun is the subject of the clause or it shows possession, the relative pronoun is required. When it is the object, it is usually optional.

Subject of clause (relative pronouns *that*, *which*, or *who* required)
People **who / that** are concerned with the effects of pesticides on the environment are buying organic produce.
Social exercise programs **that / which** offer fun group workouts are on the rise.

Showing possession (relative pronoun *whose* required)
More professionals **whose** managers allow it are opting to telecommute, or work from home.

Object of clause (relative pronouns *that*, *which*, *who*, or *whom* optional)
Hybrid cars are an option (**that / which**) more people are choosing.
Some elementary schools now offer classes for children (**who / whom / that**) they once considered too young.

GRAMMAR PLUS *see page 118*

A Look at the Starting Point on page 54 again. In which sentences is the relative pronoun required?

B Choose the sentences in which the relative pronoun is optional. Which sentences are true for your community?

☐ 1. Young families who dream of owning a house are finding they can't afford one.

☐ 2. The pressure that students feel to succeed in school is increasing.

☐ 3. People who used to go to theaters to watch movies now watch them at home.

☐ 4. People want exercise programs that are designed for their specific age group.

☐ 5. People are devoting more time to others who are less fortunate.

☐ 6. People are recycling many things which they would have thrown away in the past.

☐ 7. A lot of people who have grown tired of city life are moving to the country.

☐ 8. More college students are choosing majors that they think will lead to high-paying jobs.

C Is the relative pronoun in these sentences the subject of the clause (*S*), the object of the clause (*O*), or does it show possession (*P*)? Write the correct letter.

____ 1. Is the number of young people **who** opt for cosmetic surgery growing or shrinking?

____ 2. Who are some celebrities **whose** style has affected fashion or other trends?

____ 3. How have the foods **that** fast-food restaurants offer changed in recent years?

____ 4. What brand names **that** once were very popular are no longer as relevant?

____ 5. Are there any alternative therapies **that** you think are ineffective or even dangerous?

____ 6. Is it becoming more difficult for people **who** don't speak a foreign language fluently to get a job?

D Pair work Interview each other using the questions in part C.

4 VOCABULARY & SPEAKING
Antonyms with prefixes

A The antonyms of these adjectives can be formed by adding the prefix *il-*, *im-*, *in-*, or *ir-*. Write the correct prefix in front of each adjective.

a. ____considerate   c. ____decisive   e. ____mature   g. ____responsible

b. ____consistent   d. ____logical   f. ____proper   h. ____tolerant

B Complete each opinion with one of the antonyms in part A. Write the correct letter.

1. "You can be 40 and still be ____ if you refuse to grow up and have the expected behavior for a person your age."

2. "People today just don't care about following correct rules or manners. They have such ____ behavior."

3. "Today's politicians are so ____. They just change their opinions and statements from one day to the next."

4. "Selfish people are often ____ of others and don't care about their feelings."

5. "____ people refuse to accept ideas and behavior different from their own."

6. "Many accidents happen when people are ____ and don't give careful thought to the results of their actions."

7. "Because young people lack wisdom and reason, they often make ____ decisions."

8. "Many young people are ____ about their future and unable to choose a course of action."

C Pair work Do you agree with the opinions? Discuss with a partner.

VOCABULARY PLUS *see page 136*

5 LISTENING
Generation Y

 A Listen to a presentation by a corporate executive about two generations of employees. What audience is the presentation addressed to? What is the purpose?

B Listen again. Write the attitudes Generation Y has regarding each area in the chart. Then write what the company is planning to do to address each attitude.

	Generation Y's attitude	Plan
1. work and free time		
2. relationship to boss		
3. community involvement		

WRITING

Writing about a personal experience

A personal-experience composition usually begins with an introductory paragraph containing a thesis statement and some observations or comments. The body of the composition provides background information and gives details about what happened. The conclusion usually restates the thesis and presents the writer's feelings.

A Underline the thesis statement. Then read the composition and answer the questions below. Compare answers with a partner.

> Last month I took a giant step and finally moved to a new apartment. I had been sharing a two-bedroom apartment for two years with a friend who I'd known since childhood, and I decided that it was time to have my own place. In the beginning, I was a little scared because I would be assuming a great deal of financial responsibility. I was also a little concerned about feeling lonely, but I knew it was important to have the experience of being totally on my own.
>
> The first thing I wanted to do before making a final decision was to talk things over with my roommate. We had first moved in together because neither of us could afford . . .
>
> I looked at many apartments before making up my mind. I finally found one that I liked – an affordable one-bedroom in very good shape, with a lot of light. The apartment is . . .
>
> My new apartment is beginning to look like a home now. I've been looking at a lot of interior design websites, and I've managed to decorate my apartment. . . .
>
> Looking back, I definitely think that I made the right decision. I feel really good about having a place I can call my own. I feel more independent and responsible. Sometimes I feel a little lonely, but for the most part, I enjoy the privacy.

1. What observations or personal comments does the writer make in the first paragraph?
2. What details and background information does the body of the composition provide?
3. What additional information do you think the writer gives to complete the body paragraphs?

B Write a composition about something that has happened to you recently. Make sure to include an introductory paragraph, three body paragraphs with details, and a conclusion.

C **Pair work** Exchange papers and answer these questions.

1. Does your partner's introductory paragraph have a thesis statement?
2. Do all the details in the body of the composition support the thesis statement?
3. What other points or examples could be added?

LESSON B ▶ *A change for the better*

1 STARTING POINT
Contemplating a change

A Pair work Read about the changes these people are thinking about. Do you think they'd be happy if they made the changes? Why or why not?

My public-relations job is secure and high paying. Still, I feel as though something is missing. My real passion is skiing, and today I saw an ad for a PR consultant at a ski resort. It seems like the job was made for me! I'd have to take a big pay cut, but it might be worth it.

My parents expect me to go to a four-year college the way they did. I'm not really sure that's for me. I mean, why go away for an education when there are so many online courses? It's as if my computer is a university! For some jobs I'm interested in, I only need a professional certificate, which I could earn online in less than a year.

I'm making ends meet thanks to my part-time jobs, but I guess I'm looking for more meaning in my life. I'm thinking of joining a volunteer program to help build houses for the needy as a few of my friends have. I'd get to travel, meet new people, and do something for others.

B Group work Tell your group about a change you are thinking of making. Respond to each other's ideas with advice about the changes and other suggestions.

"I'm thinking about changing careers and getting into fashion design."

"That's cool! Maybe taking online courses in fashion would be a good place to start."

2 LISTENING
Volunteering for a change

A You are going to listen to Jody speak to Mr. Turner about volunteering in a program called Houses for All. What kind of program do you think it is?

◀)) **B** Now listen to the conversation. Which of these things is Jody concerned about? Choose the correct answers.

☐ airfare ☐ food ☐ making friends
☐ culture shock ☐ job skills ☐ visiting home

◀)) **C** Listen again. Write the three ways that Jody is hoping to benefit from the program.

1. _____

2. _____

3. _____

GRAMMAR

As if, as though, as, the way, and *like*

As if and *as though* often introduce clauses that describe impressions about feelings or behavior after verbs such as *act, behave, feel, look, seem,* and *talk*.
Still, I feel **as if / as though** something is missing.

As and *the way* introduce clauses that express a comparison.
I'm thinking of joining a volunteer program to help build houses for the needy **as / the way** a few of my friends have.

In informal English, the word *like* can be used instead of *as if / as though* and *as / the way*.
It seems **as though** the job was made for me!
It seems **like** the job was made for me!

GRAMMAR PLUS *see page 119*

A Look at the Starting Point on page 58 again. Can you find another expression you can rewrite with *like*?

B Rewrite these sentences to make them more formal using *as if, as though, as,* or *the way*. Compare your answers with a partner. More than one answer is possible.

1. Lately, I'm trying to think more positively, like I did when I was younger.
   Lately, I'm trying to think more positively, the way I did when I was younger.

2. My father is trying to exercise more like his doctor advised.

3. Sometimes I feel like the world is changing too fast.

4. To become a better listener, listen to people like everything they say is important.

5. My uncle needs to stop dressing like time has stood still for 20 years.

6. A friend of mine is teaching me to bake bread like they do in France.

C Pair work Complete these sentences so that they are true for you. Add another sentence with your own information, and compare with a partner.

1. I feel as though I don't have enough time to . . .
   cook healthy food.

2. I don't feel the need to . . . as so many people do these days.

3. Young people today feel as though . . .

4. I wish I could still . . . the way I used to when I was younger.

5. People today would find it difficult to . . . as was necessary long ago.

6. _____

D Group work Join another pair and share your answers. Ask for more specific information, and give your opinions.

"I really feel as if I don't have enough time to cook healthy food."
"What makes you say that?"
"Well, I'm so busy that there's too little time to go food shopping and make proper meals. It's easier just to grab fast food."

Useful expressions

Asking for more specific information
What makes you say that?
Why do you think that?
In what way(s)?

---

4 VOCABULARY & SPEAKING
Collocations with *change*

A Look at the expressions with *change*. Match each expression with its definition.

1. anticipate ____		a. experience a change
2. avoid ____		b. expect a change
3. bring about ____		c. successfully deal with a change
4. cope with ____	(a) change	d. fight against a change
5. go through ____		e. escape or stay away from a change
6. resist ____		f. cause a change
7. welcome ____		g. invite and be happy about a change

B **Pair work** Use the expressions to discuss with your partner changes you would (not) . . .

1. avoid.   2. be able to cope with.   3. resist.   4. welcome.   5. bring about if you could.

"I'd try to avoid changes to my current lifestyle. I'm really happy with my life right now."

"That's good to hear. But would you also avoid changes that could make your life even better?"

VOCABULARY PLUS *see page 136*

5 DISCUSSION
How do you cope?

A Complete the survey. How true is each statement for you? Choose a number from 1 to 5. Then discuss the survey with a partner.

DO YOU RESIST OR WELCOME CHANGE?	Not true at all	◄——————►			Very true
1. I set realistic goals for myself and take steps to achieve them.	1	2	3	4	5
2. I am a curious person and enjoy new experiences.	1	2	3	4	5
3. I live in the present, appreciate the past, and focus on the future.	1	2	3	4	5
4. I listen to others and seek understanding.	1	2	3	4	5
5. When solving a problem, I seek advice and support from friends and family I trust.	1	2	3	4	5
6. I am highly flexible and easygoing.	1	2	3	4	5
7. I am creative and brainstorm solutions to challenges.	1	2	3	4	5
8. I stand up for myself and say "no" when I need to.	1	2	3	4	5
9. When I fail at something, I see it as a learning experience.	1	2	3	4	5
10. I try to find humor in all situations.	1	2	3	4	5

SCORE	10–20	21–30	31–40	41–50
	You tend to avoid change. You need to learn to welcome change in your life.	You often resist change. Friends and family can help you cope with it.	You respond to change well. However, there is always room for improvement.	You are exceptionally adaptable. You bring about positive changes in your life.

B **Pair work** Think of a big change in your life. Tell your partner about your feelings and reactions at the time and how your life today is different because of it.

"Getting my driver's license was a welcome change. I felt independent and was thrilled to finally be able to go where I wanted when I wanted. . . ."

A **Pair work** Would you reduce your income by half in exchange for more free time and less stress? Discuss with a partner. Then read the article.

LEAVING THE
Rat Race
FOR THE
Simple Life

Time is more precious than money for an increasing number of people who are choosing to live more with less – and welcoming the change.

Kay and Charles Giddens, a paralegal and a trial lawyer, respectively, sold their home to start a bed and breakfast. Four years later, the couple was dishing out banana pancake breakfasts, cleaning toilets, and serving homemade chocolate chip cookies to guests in a bed and breakfast surrounded by trees on a mesa known for colorful sunsets.

"Do I miss the freeways? Do I miss the traffic? Do I miss the stress? No," said Ms. Giddens. "This is a phenomenon that's fairly widespread. A lot of people are re-evaluating their lives and figuring out what they want to do."

Simple living ranges from cutting down on weeknight activities to sharing housing, living closer to work and commuting less, avoiding shopping malls, borrowing books from the library instead of buying them, and taking a cut in pay to work at a more pleasurable job.

Vicki Robin, a writer, tells us how she copes with the changes in her budget, now far less than she used to make.

"You become conscious about where your money is going and how valuable it is," Ms. Robin says. "You tend not to use things up. You cook at home rather than eat out. Your life is less frazzled, and you discover your expenses have gone way down."

Janet Luhrs, a lawyer, quit her practice after giving birth and leaving her daughter with a nanny for two weeks. "It was not the way I wanted to raise my kids," she says. "Simplicity is not just about saving money, it's about me sitting down every night with my kids to a candlelit dinner with classical music."

Mrs. Luhrs started editing a magazine called *Simple Living* and publishing tips on how to buy recycled furniture and shoes, organize potluck dinners instead of fancy receptions, and advocating changes in consumption patterns.

"It's not about poverty or deprivation," Mrs. Luhrs explains. "It's about conscious living and creating the life you want. The less stuff you buy, the less money goes out the door, and the less money you have to earn."

Source: "Living the Simple Life – and Loving It," by Julia Duin, The Washington Times

B Complete the summary of the article. Fill in each blank with words or phrases from the article.

Many people have come to think that time is (1) _____ than money.
The Giddenses gave up their law careers to run a (2) _____, and they are
happy they did. Others have chosen to simplify their lives by (3) _____ their
activities and expenses. Janet Luhrs quit her job as a lawyer to spend more time with
(4) _____. She started editing a (5) _____ called *Simple
Living*. She understands that the less stuff you (6) _____, the less
(7) _____ you need to earn.

C **Group work** Discuss these questions. Then share your answers with the class.

1. Do you think the people in the article have improved their lives? Why?
2. What changes would you make to live more simply? How would these changes simplify your life?

8 CONSUMER CULTURE

LESSON A ▶ *What's new on the market?*

1 STARTING POINT
Smart shoppers

A Pair work Read about these four ways to find bargains. Which ones have you or your partner tried?

$MART $HOPPERS
How do you find the best bargains?

Rick, 24
"I'm really into online auctions. Members sell each other all kinds of stuff. I really get excited about the bidding – sometimes there's lots of competition. But sometimes you're the only bidder. See this hat? It only cost me two dollars!"

Carla, 32
"When I go shopping, I use this cool sale-locator app. It provides information about in-store sales to bargain hunters free of charge. The app collects information from thousand of stores, and you can also send information about deals you find to other shoppers."

Norma, 21
"Do you get tired of clothes quickly? Do you always want to buy something new for yourself? Let me give you a tip. I buy secondhand clothes at thrift shops. I can always find something I like – even designer brands – at a greatly reduced price!"

Ling Wei, 43
"For food and everyday items, I recommend wholesale clubs to everyone I know. For a small membership fee, you can go to a big warehouse-like store that sells everything in bulk – in large quantities. The rule there is: the more you buy, the more you save."

B Pair work What other ways do you find bargains? Can you remember an item you bought at a reduced price?

"There are some great discount websites that sell electronics, and you can find some awesome bargains. I got a great camera for half price from one of those sites."

2 LISTENING
Shopping preferences

A Listen to Ben and Anna talk about shopping online and in stores. Choose their preference and write three positive aspects they mention about it.

	Ben		Anna	
Shopping preference	☐ online	☐ in stores	☐ online	☐ in stores
Positive aspects				
Negative aspects				

B Listen again. Write two negative aspects they mention in the chart.

C Pair work Do you prefer shopping online or in stores? Explain your preference.

GRAMMAR

Placement of direct and indirect objects

For most verbs in English, including *get, give, lend, offer, sell, send, show, teach,* and *tell,* direct and indirect objects follow these patterns:

Pattern A
direct object + *to / for* + indirect object
You can send **information to other shoppers**.
You can send **information to them**.
You can send **it to other shoppers**.
You can send **it to them**.

Pattern B
indirect object + direct object
You can send **other shoppers information**.
You can send **them information**.

With verbs such as *announce, describe, explain, mention, provide, recommend, return,* and *say,* the indirect object cannot precede the direct object. Sentences follow Pattern A above.
It provides **information** about in-store sales **to bargain hunters** free of charge.
It provides **it to them** free of charge.

With verbs such as *allow, ask, cause,* and *cost,* the indirect object precedes the direct object and takes no preposition. Sentences follow Pattern B above.
It only cost **Rick two dollars**!
It only cost **him two dollars**!

GRAMMAR PLUS *see page 120*

A Look at the Starting Point on page 62 again. Find more sentences containing both a direct and an indirect object. Which pattern do they follow?

B Complete these sentences using the words in parentheses. Whenever possible, write the sentence in two different ways.

1. Many companies use cartoon characters to sell . . . (products / children)
   products to children. / children products.

2. If I'm not satisfied with a product, I never hesitate to return . . . (it / the store)

3. The Internet has made shopping much easier, but delivery costs . . . (more money / people)

4. At restaurants, my wife thinks I ask . . . (too many questions / the waiter)

5. At discount stores, when they lower prices, they always announce . . . (it / the shoppers)

6. When I told the baker the bread smelled good, he gave . . . (a free sample / me)

7. In most malls, there is a directory that shows . . . (the locations of all the stores / the shoppers)

8. Good salespeople convincingly explain . . . (the benefits of a product / their customers)

C Pair work Use the verbs below to talk about things you've bought recently. Ask follow-up questions.

ask	describe	give	return
cost	explain	recommend	tell

"A friend recommended a new discount store to me, and I finally went there last weekend."
"What kinds of things do they sell?"
"Mainly high-tech electronics and stuff like that."
"Did you buy anything?"
"Yeah. I bought a toy robot for my nephew."

Shopping experiences

A Pair work Match each expression with its meaning. Then compare with a partner.

1. go over your credit limit _g_
2. be a bargain hunter ____
3. be a compulsive shopper ____
4. have buyer's remorse ____
5. make an impulse buy ____
6. bid on an item ____
7. go on a shopping spree ____
8. go window-shopping ____

a. have regrets after making an unwise purchase
b. be unable to control your need to buy things
c. buy something suddenly without having planned to
d. spend lots of money shopping for pleasure
e. look at goods in stores without buying any
f. be a person who looks for low-priced products
g. charge more to your credit card than the allowed amount
h. offer money to buy an item at an auction

B Group work Which of these experiences related to shopping have you had? Share your experiences with the group. Use the expressions in part A where appropriate.

- You made an impulse buy.
- You resisted buying something you wanted.
- You bought something and later wished you hadn't.

"I'm usually a bargain hunter, but this outfit looked so good on the store mannequin that I just had to buy it."

VOCABULARY PLUS see page 137

DISCUSSION

Are you a compulsive shopper?

A Pair work Which statements are true for you? Choose *yes* or *no* for each statement. Then discuss your answers with a partner.

What Are Your **SHOPPING HABITS?**	Yes	No
1. I can never go shopping without making an impulse buy.	O	O
2. I often buy things that I end up never wearing or using.	O	O
3. At home, I frequently feel tempted to go online and buy something.	O	O
4. When I visit a new city, I spend most of my free time shopping.	O	O
5. I always have buyer's remorse after going on a shopping spree.	O	O
6. I have gone over my credit limit at least once.	O	O
7. As soon as new fashions appear in the stores, I have to buy them.	O	O
8. After buying things, I sometimes lie to relatives and friends about the price.	O	O
9. I sometimes go shopping to forget my troubles.	O	O

B Group work Discuss these questions. Then share your ideas with the class.

1. What are some other characteristics of a compulsive shopper?
2. What other problems do compulsive shoppers face?
3. What would you do to help a compulsive shopper?

6 WRITING
Supporting an opinion

> When writing a composition that supports an opinion, first present the opinion in the thesis statement. Then support it in subsequent paragraphs with examples and details.

A Read the composition and discuss your answers to the questions.

1. What is the writer's opinion?
2. What are the reasons given to support the opinion?

    Having almost unlimited credit is certainly one of the many advantages of using credit cards. However, this benefit can easily turn into a major problem. With unlimited credit, people spend too much money. I think there should be a limit to the total amount of credit people can have. This way, the total amount of credit on all of their credit cards together could never go over a certain percentage of their income.

    Many compulsive shoppers run up such high debts that they go bankrupt, creating problems for their families as well as for the people to whom they owe money. Currently, it is easy for people to accumulate many credit cards. Although the credit cards have limits, the number of credit cards is not limited. People with 10 credit cards, each with a $5,000 limit, have $50,000 of credit, even though they might not be able to pay all of their bills. Such a situation can quickly lead to bankruptcy.

    People need to be given an absolute credit limit. If people were not permitted to go over this limit, they would have to be more responsible with their money and evaluate which purchases were most important to them. I think that the actual limit on credit card spending should be based on income so that credit would be based on the ability to pay.

B Complete one of these opinions on shopping or use one of your own. Then present your opinion in a thesis statement.

1. No one under 18 should be allowed to . . .
2. People with a lot of debt should . . .
3. Stores should never give cash refunds for . . .
4. Customers who break an item in a store should . . .
5. Shoplifters should do community service by . . .

C Make a list of details or examples to support your thesis statement. Then write a composition with an introductory paragraph containing your opinion, and at least one paragraph with supporting examples or details.

D **Pair work** Take turns reading each other's compositions. Can you think of additional examples or details your partner could use to be more persuasive?

LESSON B ▶ *Consumer awareness*

1 STARTING POINT
Print advertisements

A Pair work Look at the three advertisements. Which kind do you think is the most effective? Where else do you see advertisements?

magazine ads　　　　　　　*company logos*　　　　　　　*billboards*

B Pair work Read these opinions about advertisements. Do you agree with them? What do you think makes a good advertisement?

- "I think consumers need to insist that advertisements be truthful in every respect."
- "It seems to me that a good ad is a memorable ad – one that sticks in your head."
- "I believe it is essential that an ad be clever and witty in order to be effective."
- "Some ads seem to demand that the customer buy the product. I don't like a 'hard-sell' approach."
- "I think it's crucial that an ad clearly communicate the benefits of the product it is selling."

2 LISTENING
Radio ads

A Pair work What types of products or services are typically advertised on the radio? Do you think radio is an effective advertising medium?

◀)) B Listen to three radio advertisements. What products are they for? Write the name and type of each product in the chart in part C.

◀)) C Listen again. What benefits of the products are highlighted in the ads? Complete the chart.

	Name of product	Type of product	Benefit(s)
1.			
2.			
3.			

GRAMMAR

Verbs in the subjunctive

Certain expressions and verbs such as *demand*, *insist*, *propose*, *recommend*, *request*, and *suggest* are followed by the subjunctive. The subjunctive uses the base form of the verb. It is generally used in formal language to express a wish or necessity.

I think consumers need to insist (that) **advertisements be** truthful in every respect.
Some ads seem to demand (that) **the customer buy** the product.

These expressions are frequently followed by the subjunctive:

it is crucial	it is imperative	it is important
it is essential	it is vital	it is critical

I believe it is essential that **an ad be** clever and witty in order to be effective.

GRAMMAR PLUS *see page 121*

A Look at the Starting Point on page 66 again. Which opinion does not use the subjunctive?

B Use verbs followed by the subjunctive instead of *should* or *must* to rewrite these sentences without changing the meaning.

1. Companies should advertise more to increase sales. (I / suggest)
   I suggest that companies advertise more to increase sales.
2. Advertising agencies should use humor in their ads. (It is important)
3. Cities should tear down billboards that obstruct city views. (I / demand)
4. The government must regulate ads on the Internet. (It is essential)
5. Viewers should skip the ads that precede online video clips. (I / recommend)
6. The advertising of harmful products must stop. (It is crucial)
7. False advertising should be treated as a serious crime. (I / propose)
8. Public television should remain commercial free. (It is vital)

C Group work Use the verbs and expressions in the box below to give these people advice on their problems. Do you ever have similar problems? Ask your group for advice.

insist	it is crucial	it is essential
propose	recommend	suggest

Useful expressions

Asking for advice

What do you think I should do?
What would you do if you were me?
What would you do if you were in my position?

❶ "The fast food in commercials and posters always looks great. It looks so good I can't resist buying some, but what they actually give me looks pretty bad and really unappetizing."

❷ "I saw a clothing store with a big 'Going Out of Business' sign in the window last year, so I went in and bought a lot of clothes. Now, it's a year later, and the sign is still there."

❸ "Several friends told me they have received spam emails from me offering to sell them diet pills. The thing is, I didn't send the emails. Someone must have hacked my email account!"

VOCABULARY
Marketing strategies

A Look at the list of marketing strategies. Write the correct letter to complete the sentences below.

a. a free sample   d. comparative marketing   g. a loyalty program

b. coupon codes   e. search-engine marketing   h. word-of-mouth marketing

c. product placement   f. a celebrity endorsement

1. ____ gets attention for products when they are shown in movies or on TV shows.

2. ____ links the name and image of a famous person to a product.

3. ____ lets people try a product they weren't planning on buying.

4. ____ promotes a product or service related to your search on the results page.

5. ____ rewards customers for repeatedly purchasing products from one retailer.

6. ____ occurs when satisfied customers tell others about their positive experience.

7. ____ can be obtained at many websites and entitle customers to discounts.

8. ____ points out the superiority of a product over its competitors.

B **Pair work** With your partner, brainstorm an example from real life for as many of the marketing strategies as you can. How effective do you think they were?

VOCABULARY PLUS *see page 137*

DISCUSSION
The ethics of undercover marketing

A **Pair work** Look at the expressions in Exercise 4. Which of them describe undercover marketing strategies, in which people are not aware that they are being marketed to? Discuss your answers with your partner.

B **Group work** Read about undercover marketing. Then discuss the questions below with your group.

Undercover marketers (also called "stealth marketers") try to find ways to introduce products to people without actually letting them know that they are being marketed to. Here are three actual techniques that have been used for undercover marketing.

The product is a video gaming glove that allows gamers to control games with small finger movements. Unknown actors go into coffee shops and enthusiastically use the glove. This attracts interested people. The actor lets them try it out, never saying who he is.

A top cell phone company sent 60 actors to 10 cities with its latest model. The actors pretended to be tourists and asked people to take their picture with the phone. In this way, they put the new phone in people's hands and let them interact with it.

To attract attention and appear well established, a young firm had fake newspapers printed that had full back-page ads for the company. They then paid people to ride the subways in a major city, pretending to read the newspapers while holding up the ads for all to see.

1. Which of these three marketing techniques seems the most unethical to you? Why?

2. Do you think undercover marketing should be controlled by the government? Why or why not?

A Pair work What influences you most to try a new brand or product? How likely are you to use the same brands and products your friends use? Discuss with a partner. Then read the article.

Word-of-Mouth MARKETING

It was close to midnight as one truck after another crept down a quiet street in Laguna Beach, one of the most beautiful, affluent, and expensive communities in Southern California. Considering the time of night, it was unusual to see vehicles on the road. Yet several trucks stood silhouetted in the driveway and along the front curb as workers silently unloaded camera equipment and cardboard boxes, and then carried them inside the Morgenson family home.

What took place over the next eight weeks was inspired by a Hollywood movie called *The Joneses* about a family of stealth marketers who move into an upper-middle-class neighborhood to **peddle** their wares to unsuspecting neighbors. The idea was both simple and ambitious: to test the power of word-of-mouth marketing. By filming a "real" family in spontaneous, unscripted situations, my team and I would document how the Morgensons' circle of friends responded to specific brands and products the Morgensons brought into their lives. Would they want all the things that family has? Would this influence be so powerful as to make them actually go out and buy those things?

With the help of 35 video cameras and 25 microphones **tucked away** inside the furniture and fixtures, the clandestine operation revealed something shocking. The most powerful hidden persuader of all isn't in your TV or on the shelves of your supermarket or even lurking in your smartphones. It's a far more **pervasive** influence that's around you virtually every waking moment: your very own friends and neighbors. There's nothing quite so persuasive as observing someone we respect or admire using a brand or product.

Our analysis also found that the brands the Morgensons advocated went viral faster. Roughly one third of the Morgensons' friends began promoting these same brands to *their* friends and acquaintances. We also found that the brands their peers were most likely to buy at the Morgensons' subtle suggestion were the bigger and better-known ones. This confirmed my theory that conventional marketing and the more **covert** variety work well together. The most persuasive advertising strategies become that much more so when **amplified** by word-of-mouth advertising.

Whenever I meet with company executives, I remind them that the people who hold the *real* marketing power are **hyperconnected**, mouse-clicking consumers and their wide circles of virtual and real-life friends and acquaintances. In other words, the people who hold the real power are *us*.

Source: "Word-of-Mouth Marketing: We All Want to Keep Up with the Joneses," by Martin Lindstrom

B Pair work Write the expressions and words in boldface from the article next to their meanings.

1. undercover _____
2. strengthened _____
3. hidden _____
4. sell _____
5. always online _____
6. widespread and invasive _____

C Group work Discuss these questions. Then share your answers with the class.

1. In your opinion, what were the most interesting findings of the experiment described in the article?

2. Do you agree that there's nothing quite as persuasive as seeing people we admire and respect using a brand or product? Why or why not?

3. How ethical do you think covert word-of-mouth marketing is? Does the experiment described in the article present any dilemmas or limitations? Explain.

1 STARTING POINT
Amazing animals

A Read about these three famous animals. Have you heard of any of them before? Which do you think is the most impressive?

Ruby

Ruby was one of many elephants that learned to paint at the Phoenix Zoo. Wherever there are elephants painting, people are fascinated. Ruby was even more intriguing because she chose her own colors when she painted. Her works raised about $500,000 for the zoo.

Bart the Bear

Bart the Bear was a nine-foot Alaskan Kodiak bear. When he was a cub, he was raised by humans and trained to act in films. Whenever actors worked with him, they were always impressed. He worked with stars such as Brad Pitt and Steven Seagal.

Alex

Alex's name is usually mentioned whenever experts talk about language use by animals. It is claimed that this African grey parrot could categorize about 150 words, count numbers, and distinguish colors and shapes. He showed some of his skills on several nature shows on TV.

B Pair work Discuss these questions and share your ideas with the class.

1. Do you think animals should be trained for entertainment? Is it ethical?
2. What other interesting talents or skills do animals have?

"I think it's OK to train animals as performers, provided they don't suffer in any way when trained."

2 LISTENING
Helping hands

◄)) **A** Listen to these news reports on animals that help people. What kinds of people does each animal help?

◄)) **B** Listen again. How does each animal help the people? Write *M* for monkey, *D* for dog, or *NG* for information not given.

____ 1. fetching objects

____ 2. picking things up off the floor

____ 3. helping them to cross streets

____ 4. taking them places

____ 5. doing tricks to make them laugh

____ 6. sparking memories of pets

____ 7. giving them something to take care of

____ 8. scratching an itchy nose

____ 9. giving them something to look forward to

3 GRAMMAR

Whenever and *wherever* contrasted with *when* and *where*

Whenever and *wherever* mean "at any time" and "in any place." They are used to introduce adverbial clauses. Notice their position in the sentences.
Whenever experts talk about language use by animals, Alex's name is usually mentioned.
Alex's name is usually mentioned **whenever experts talk about language use by animals**.
Wherever there are elephants painting, people are fascinated.
People are fascinated **wherever there are elephants painting**.

When and *where* can replace *whenever* and *wherever* when they have the sense of "at any time" or "in any place."
Whenever / When actors worked with Bart the Bear, they were always impressed.
Wherever / Where there are elephants painting, people are fascinated.

Whenever and *wherever* cannot be used if the sentence refers to a specific time or location.
In these cases, *when* and *where* are used.
Whenever actors worked with him, they were always impressed. *(any time)*
When Brad Pitt worked with Bart in *Legends of the Fall*, he was very impressed. *(specific time)*
Wherever there are elephants painting, people are fascinated. *(any place)*
There were a lot of people **where** the elephants were painting today. *(specific place)*

GRAMMAR PLUS *see page 122*

A Look at the Starting Point on page 70 again. In which sentences can *whenever* and *wherever* be used interchangeably with *when* and *where*?

B Complete the sentences with *whenever* or *wherever*.
If the time or place is specific, use *when* or *where*.

1. Large animals, like tigers and bears, need to be trained
   _____ they are still very young.

2. Though large, trained elephants are obedient. They will
   usually go _____ they are led.

3. _____ someone has an unusual pet,
   serious problems can arise.

4. _____ you see a cat flatten its ears,
   you should assume it's upset.

5. _____ my sister and her family live now,
   tenants aren't allowed to have pets.

6. _____ a messenger pigeon is taken
   somewhere and released, it almost always find its way home.

C Match the clauses on the left with clauses on the right. Make logical sentences
using *when, whenever, where,* or *wherever*.

1. We were very startled last night _c_
2. Parrots become very sad ____
3. The sheep population grows quickly ____
4. A guide dog always stops ____
5. Police officers ride horses ____
6. Our helper monkey wakes us up ____

a. the traffic light is red.
b. cars can't conveniently go.
c. a bat flew into the window.
d. there is plenty of grass to eat.
e. the sun comes up in the morning.
f. they are separated from their owners.

We were very startled last night when a bat flew into the window.

4 VOCABULARY
Physical features of animals

A Pair work Look at this list of animal features. Which type(s) of animal do they belong to? Write them in the correct column(s) in the chart.

beaks	fangs	fins	gills	horns	scales	tusks
claws	feathers	fur	hooves	paws	tails	wings

Birds	Fish	Reptiles	Mammals

B Pair work Which animal features in part A do people make use of? Which animals do they come from, and what are the uses?

"Feathers are used in various ways. For example, many pillows are stuffed with duck or goose feathers."

VOCABULARY PLUS *see page 138*

5 DISCUSSION
Is it right to do that?

A Look at these ways humans use animals. How acceptable do you think they are? Add one idea of your own, and complete the chart.

ANIMAL ETHICS	I'm against it.	It depends.	I'm OK with it.
1. using ivory from elephant tusks in jewelry	☐	☐	☐
2. using rhinoceros horns for medicines	☐	☐	☐
3. using animals for medical research	☐	☐	☐
4. wearing animal fur and leather	☐	☐	☐
5. serving wild animal meat in restaurants	☐	☐	☐
6. using animals to test cosmetics	☐	☐	☐
7. training animals to perform in circuses	☐	☐	☐
8. _____	☐	☐	☐

B Group work Share your answers with the group, and explain your reasons. Who in your group seems to be the most "animal-friendly"?

"For me, using ivory from elephant tusks in jewelry depends on whether or not the ivory was taken from elephants that were killed illegally."

6 WRITING
Classification essay

A classification essay organizes information into categories. The first paragraph introduces the overall topic of the essay, includes a thesis statement, and gives an overview of the categories the writer will focus on. Each subsequent paragraph provides detailed information about one of the categories. A conclusion gives an additional perspective on the overall topic.

A Read this classification essay. What special kind of dog is the main topic of the essay? What three categories of this type of dog does the writer provide more information about?

Although most dogs offer their owners little more than companionship, assistance dogs are specially trained to assist people with disabilities or special needs. These dogs devote themselves to helping their owners live more independent lives. There are several types of assistance dogs, but the most common are guide dogs, hearing dogs, and service dogs.

Guide dogs help blind or visually impaired people get around their homes and communities. Most guide dogs are large breeds like Labrador retrievers and German shepherds, which wear a harness with a U-shaped handle to allow the dog and its human partner to communicate. The owner gives directional commands, and the dog's role is to ensure the human's safety, even if it means disobeying an unsafe command.

Hearing dogs alert a person who is deaf or hearing-impaired to sounds like doorbells, a baby's cries, and smoke alarms. They're trained to make physical contact and lead their owner to the source of the sound. Hearing dogs may be any size or breed, but they tend to be small to medium-sized mixed breeds because they are rescued from shelters. Hearing dogs can all be identified by their orange collar and vest.

Service dogs usually assist people who are confined to a wheelchair. The dogs are trained to pick up dropped objects, open and close doors, help in getting a person into or out of a wheelchair, and find help when needed. Because many of these tasks require strength, most service dogs are large breeds such as golden or Labrador retrievers. These dogs usually wear a backpack, harness, or vest.

Guide dogs, hearing dogs, and service dogs have one thing in common, however. Before being matched with a human partner, each type of assistance dog undergoes a one- to two-year training program. Once the dog and owner are matched, they begin to form a bond of trust with each other and often become an inseparable team.

B Choose one of these topics or one of your own. Brainstorm ways to classify your topic into at least three categories, and make a list of ideas for each.

- types of cats
- types of pets
- types of pet owners
- people who work with animals

C Write a classification essay that includes an introduction, three or more paragraphs – each one about a different category – and a conclusion.

D **Pair work** Read your partner's essay. Is the thesis statement clear? Are the categories distinct? Is each category described adequately? What other information would you want to have included?

1 STARTING POINT
Careers in nature

A Read the job postings on this website. Do you know anyone who has one of these jobs? What else do you know about the jobs?

Careers in Nature	about us	jobs	testimonials	search

You'll find whatever you need to start a career in nature right here!

Job title	Description	
Nature photographer	Photograph wildflowers in national parks for an exciting catalog project. Camera equipment is not provided; candidates must bring whatever they need. . . .	Details
Diving instructor	Scuba diving instructors are needed at a world-class resort to lead underwater tours. Extra consideration will be given to whoever can start immediately. . . .	Details
Landscape architect	Join our team and help design and implement landscape plans on university campuses. Whoever applies should have at least five years of experience. . . .	Details
Wildlife rehabilitator	Be ready to do whatever is required to return injured animals to the wild. Take care of orphaned animals and assist veterinarians with post-operative care. . . .	Details
Naturalist	Lead children on educational nature walks. Whoever enjoys explaining things and has a love for the outdoors might be right for this position. . . .	Details

B Pair work Choose one of the jobs on the website or another nature-related job you might be interested in trying. Tell your partner what interests you about it.

2 LISTENING
An eco-resort

A Listen to a conversation with the manager of an eco-resort. Who is the manager speaking with? Choose the correct answer.

☐ a guest   ☐ a job applicant   ☐ a journalist   ☐ a nature guide

B Listen again. What is special about these features of the eco-resort? Complete the chart.

Eco-resort feature	Reasons it is special
1. Resort design	
2. Nature guides	
3. Spa	
4. Zip lines	

C Pair work If you were designing an eco-resort, which of the features in part B would you include in your resort? Why? What other features would you include?

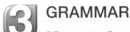

3 GRAMMAR

Noun clauses with *whoever* and *whatever*

Whoever and *whatever* can begin noun clauses and function as either the subject or object of the clause.

Whoever = the person who / anyone who / everyone who
Whoever applies should have at least five years of experience.
Extra consideration will be given to **whoever** can start immediately.

Whatever = anything that / everything that
Be ready to do **whatever** is required to return injured animals to the wild.
You'll find **whatever** you need to start a career in nature right here!

GRAMMAR PLUS *see page 123*

A Look at the Starting Point on page 74 again. In which sentences are *whoever* or *whatever* used as the subject of a clause? In which are they the object of a clause?

B Complete the sentences with *whoever* or *whatever*. Then compare your answers with a partner.

1. Here's a warning to _____ is thinking about becoming a beekeeper: You *will* be stung!

2. The birds on that island are curious about people and approach _____ they see coming.

3. Nature photographers take pictures of landscapes and _____ they see in the wild.

4. It's a forest ranger's duty to immediately report _____ looks like smoke or fire.

5. _____ took this photo of Mount Everest is a talented nature photographer.

6. I'm sure a relaxing trip to the mountains will take your mind off _____ is bothering you.

7. Visitors must follow the rules and are not allowed to do _____ they want in nature reserves.

8. Wildflowers are protected by law in many places; _____ picks them is subject to a fine.

C Group work Complete the statements with your own ideas. Compare and discuss your ideas with your group.

1. Whoever has a strong desire to help animals . . .
   should consider volunteering some of their time at a wildlife center.
2. Whatever humans really need is provided by nature. For example, people can get . . .
3. Hiking is a great pastime for whoever . . .
4. It's a bad idea to feed a pet whatever it wants. Instead, . . .
5. Whoever is planning an excursion in nature . . .

4 VOCABULARY
Nature-related idioms

A Match the idioms in boldface with their meanings.

1. Her ideas are **a breath of fresh air** among so many outdated ones. __e__
2. Our contribution to the wildlife fund was just **a drop in the ocean**, but even small donations help. ____
3. His report on the wildfire is **as clear as mud**. I can't understand it. ____
4. This project is **a walk in the park**. The other one was so complex. ____
5. These are just initial ideas for the campaign. Nothing is **set in stone**. ____
6. This is just **the tip of the iceberg**. Things are much worse than that. ____
7. My son is **under the weather** today, so he can't go on the field trip. ____
8. The plans are still **up in the air**. Nothing has been decided yet. ____

a. easy
b. confusing; unclear
c. unchangeable
d. not feeling well
e. new, different, exciting
f. less/fewer than needed
g. undecided; uncertain
h. a small perceptible part of a much bigger problem

B Pair work Use the idioms to talk to your partner about nature-related issues.

"The new plan of turning that run-down area of the city into a park is a breath of fresh air. The previous plans were not very interesting."

VOCABULARY PLUS see page 138

5 DISCUSSION
The importance of nature

A How in touch with nature are you? Complete the survey to find out.

Are You in Touch with Nature?

	Agree	⟷	Disagree
1. Human beings are a part of nature, and therefore must interact frequently with nature to be healthy.	2	1	0
2. It's important to work or study in a space with indoor plants and large windows that let in sunlight.	2	1	0
3. Everyone needs at least one hobby, such as horseback riding or gardening, to keep in touch with nature.	2	1	0
4. When it comes to clothing and body care, it's best to wear natural fibers and use natural soaps and shampoos.	2	1	0
5. When I'm under the weather, I prefer to use all-natural treatments instead of synthetic drugs.	2	1	0
6. I would have been happier living in harmony with nature in a time before industry and technology.	2	1	0
7. Given a choice, I'd buy free-range poultry and meat products. I'd also buy wild fish instead of farmed varieties.	2	1	0
8. I recycle everything I can. Although my efforts might be just a drop in the ocean, I think I'm helping to preserve our natural resources.	2	1	0

SCORE

0–4 Like much of modern society, you may be out of touch with the natural world.

5–8 While nature isn't a priority for you, you do appreciate it when you experience it.

9–12 You see nature as an important part of your life and necessary for your well-being.

13–16 You're a nature lover who needs to be in constant contact with the natural world.

B Group work Discuss your answers to the survey. Talk about the reasons for your choices and whether or not you agree with your score.

A **Pair work** What are some of the daily tasks a park ranger might have to do in a city park? Discuss with a partner. Then read the article.

A SUMMER JOB that's a **walk** in the **park**

Every summer, curious creatures infiltrate New York City's biggest parks. They number in the dozens, walk on their hind legs, are khaki in color, and exceedingly amiable by nature. Their most distinguished markings are their wide-brimmed Smokey Bear hats.

They are Urban Park Ranger fellows, possessors of what may be the best, if not the most unusual, summer jobs in New York. "It's pretty laid back – kind of therapeutic," said Mohammed Alomeri, 22, who is from Midwood, Brooklyn, and works as a summer ranger at Fort Greene Park. "Every day, literally, is a walk in the park."

The summer fellows supplement the corps of year-round Urban Park Rangers – who also wear the Smokey Bear hats, but also carry nightsticks and can issue summonses – during the parks' busiest season. ...

Daily tasks can include, but are not limited to, giving nature walks, history talks, and children's craft classes; guiding people who have gotten lost; asking people to leash their dogs; getting outdoor chefs to move their barbecue grills away from trees; talking about why feeding chicken nuggets to birds is unhealthy; explaining that, yes, they are rangers, just like the ones in national parks; and posing for tourists' cameras. ...

Rangers field hundreds of calls from park visitors who are concerned about the behavior of wildlife, often when the animals in question are behaving naturally. They get reports from people who are unnerved by the sight of raccoons, or who mistakenly assume that pigeons sunning themselves have broken wings, or who grow vexed whenever an animal wanders onto a jogging path. The sight of hawks hunting smaller birds will invariably yield dozens of concerned calls.

"They call and say, 'You gotta get in there and get that pigeon out,'" said Richard Simon, who is citywide ranger captain and oversees the fellowship program. "That's when we explain, 'This is the food chain.'" ...

The rangers also get reports about animals that truly are hurt or in the wrong place. They are handed injured baby birds, alerted to exotic animals that have been dumped by their owners, or led to stunned squirrels that have fallen from trees. "They fall out of trees all the time," said Kathy Vasquez, a full-time, year-round ranger. "They usually land on their feet, but sometimes not so much." ...

The summer rangers program ends on Saturday, which means a return to a life indoors for most of the five dozen fellows. Mr. Alomeri, however, plans to apply for a position as a full-time ranger. He has only one semester left at Brooklyn College, where he is studying physics, and wants to put off graduate school. He has fallen in love with being a ranger, and delights at the way he can now identify trees and birds. ...

Source: "A Summer Job That Promises Nature Walks for Pay," by Cara Buckley, *The New York Times* (The ellipses indicate passages omitted from the original article.)

B **Pair work** Find the words in the article that match the meanings below.

1. friendly (paragraph 1) _____
2. healing (paragraph 2) _____
3. respond to (paragraph 5) _____
4. agitated (paragraph 5) _____
5. lead to (paragraph 5) _____
6. abandoned (paragraph 7) _____

C **Group work** Discuss these questions. Then share your answers with the class.

1. How do the Urban Park Ranger fellows help park visitors connect with nature?
2. What evidence from the article might lead you to assume that many park visitors are not familiar with nature? Is the same true about city dwellers where you're from? Explain.
3. Do you agree that being an Urban Park Ranger fellow would be laid back and therapeutic? Why?

SELF-ASSESSMENT

How well can you do these things? Choose the best answer.

I can . . .	Very well	OK	A little
▸ Take part in a discussion about recent trends and life choices (Ex. 1)	☐	☐	☐
▸ Take part in a decision-making discussion about marketing a new product or service (Ex. 2)	☐	☐	☐
▸ Give a persuasive presentation about a new product or service (Ex. 2)	☐	☐	☐
▸ Take part in a discussion about animals as pets (Ex. 3)	☐	☐	☐
▸ Understand an interview about animal caretaking (Ex. 4)	☐	☐	☐

Now do the corresponding exercises. Was your assessment correct?

1 DISCUSSION
Trends and attitudes

A Pair work Read what these people have to say about some trends. Who do you agree with the most, and who do you agree with the least? Discuss your ideas with a partner, and give reasons for them.

CARLOS

"I think it's great that so many companies allow employees to telecommute. It's illogical, even irresponsible, for companies to require employees who don't live nearby to come in to work every day."

HUI LIN

"Something that worries me is the way people risk their health by experimenting with alternative medicines and therapies that haven't been properly tested. No one really knows how safe they are."

STEPHANIE

"I'm hoping attitudes toward consumption – like constantly buying new clothes – are changing. Celebrities like actors, musicians, and athletes, whom young people look up to, need to set the right example and help bring about change."

"I disagree with Hui Lin. I don't think alternative medicines are dangerous. Many of them are traditional medicines that have been used for years. However, I agree with . . ."

B Group work Discuss how you feel about these life choices. Then share your answers with the class.

- adult children returning home to live with their parents
- people choosing to get married at a later age
- people socializing more online than they do in person
- senior citizens going back to school to earn degrees
- people choosing to spend more of their free time doing volunteer work

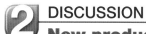

2 DISCUSSION
New products and marketing plans

A Group work Think of a new product or service you think would be successful. What is it? Who is it for? How does it work? What's the best way to advertise and promote it?

"Well, I'm thinking about a concierge service for people who are new in town. The concierge could provide the same services as a concierge in a hotel."

"I suggest we offer information and advice to help them cope with all the changes."

"Good idea. I recommend we advertise on the town's website. . . ."

B Class activity Present your product or service and marketing plans to the class. Which group has the best ideas?

3 SPEAKING
Suitable pets?

A Would you consider having any of these animals as pets? Why or why not?

tropical fish

boa constrictor

chimpanzee

B Pair work Compare your ideas with a partner. Explain your reasons.

"I really love tropical fish. Whenever I get the chance, I go snorkeling. I wouldn't have them as pets, though. I would rather see them in the ocean than in an aquarium."

4 LISTENING
Bird talk

 A Listen to an interview with a parrot expert. She mentions three things that are important for a person to have before getting an African grey parrot. Choose the three basic requirements she mentions.

- ☐ a. time
- ☐ b. videos
- ☐ c. space
- ☐ d. interest in parrots
- ☐ e. children
- ☐ f. other birds

B Listen again. Are these statements true or false? Choose the correct answer.

	True	False
1. It is illegal to import wild African grey parrots.	☐	☐
2. Parrots cause asthma.	☐	☐
3. Parrots are intelligent and unpredictable.	☐	☐
4. Parrots need some time outside of their cage each day.	☐	☐
5. Research has been done on African grey parrots talking.	☐	☐
6. Parrots can eat all fruits and vegetables.	☐	☐

10 LANGUAGE

LESSON A ▶ *Communication skills*

1 STARTING POINT
Effective communicators

A Read about these effective communicators. What else do you know about them?

Steve Jobs, the former CEO of Apple, is remembered for his contributions to communications technologies, such as smartphones and music players. Many of his design innovations are still being imitated by competitors. Jobs will also be remembered as an inspiring public speaker, as when he told Stanford University graduates: "Your time is limited, so don't waste it living someone else's life." Business presentations have been forever transformed by his simple but engaging style.

No one should have been surprised when **Nelson Mandela** was awarded the Nobel Peace Prize in 1993. Even while in prison for 27 years, his fight to end apartheid in South Africa was being kept alive by activists around the world. Mandela is always going to be remembered for his great speeches and eloquent quotations, such as, "Education is the most powerful weapon which you can use to change the world." In 2005, for his contribution to international understanding, he was designated Goodwill Ambassador by UNESCO.

B Pair work Who are some effective communicators you know? What qualities make them effective?

2 DISCUSSION
Fear of public speaking

A Studies have shown that public speaking is many people's biggest fear. Do you share this fear? Complete the survey. Add a statement of your own.

Are you AFRAID to talk?	Always true	Sometimes true	Never true
1 I can't sleep the night before a presentation.	☐	☐	☐
2 I rarely participate in discussions at work or in class.	☐	☐	☐
3 I avoid situations in which I might have to give an impromptu speech.	☐	☐	☐
4 When talking to others, I find it hard to look people in the eye.	☐	☐	☐
5 I can speak only from a prepared speech.	☐	☐	☐
6 I am intimidated by job interviews.	☐	☐	☐
7 I'd rather go to the dentist, pay taxes, or clean closets than give a presentation.	☐	☐	☐
8 _____	☐	☐	☐

Source: Schaum's Quick Guide to Great Presentation Skills

B Pair work Compare and explain your answers using examples from your life whenever possible. What do you have in common? How are you different?

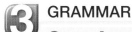

GRAMMAR

Overview of passives

Passive sentences focus on the receiver of the action by making it the subject of the sentence. The agent that performs the action can be omitted or follow *by* after the verb.

Passive = subject + form of *be* + past participle (+ *by* + agent)

Simple present: Steve Jobs **is remembered** for his contributions to communications technologies.

Present continuous: Many of his design innovations **are** still **being imitated** (by competitors).

Present perfect: Business presentations **have been** forever **transformed** by his simple but engaging style.

Simple past: Nelson Mandela **was awarded** the Nobel Peace Prize in 1993.

Past continuous: Mandela's fight **was being kept** alive (by activists) around the world.

Future with *going to*: Mandela **is** always **going to be remembered** for his great speeches.

Modals: Jobs **will** also **be remembered** as an inspiring public speaker.

Past modals: No one **should have been surprised**.

GRAMMAR PLUS *see page 124*

A Look at the Starting Point on page 80 again. Can you find another example of the passive? What verb form is it in?

B Change these active sentences to the passive. Keep or omit the agent as appropriate.

1. The Internet has changed the way the world communicates.
   The way the world communicates has been changed by the Internet.

2. People should deliver presentations confidently and cheerfully.

3. Someone should have told the students to speak louder during their speeches.

4. Counselors are advising married couples to communicate more openly.

5. Long ago, people used smoke signals to send simple messages in China.

6. After the ceremony, the president is announcing the scholarship recipients.

7. Translators are going to translate the president's speech into 35 languages.

8. The principal was making an announcement when the microphone went dead.

C Complete these sentences with information about language that is true for you. Then add another sentence of your own using a passive verb form.

1. I've been told by many people that . . .
   my English sounds quite formal.

2. My classmates and I are encouraged to . . .

3. I hope that someday I will be complimented on . . .

4. Students should / shouldn't be forced to . . .

5. Languages should be taught . . .

6. I've been advised . . .

7. Not long ago, I was told that . . .

8. _____

4 VOCABULARY
Discourse markers

A Discourse markers are expressions that make communication flow more smoothly. Match each expression below with a function it serves. Sometimes more than one answer is possible.

a. to open a presentation   c. to add information   e. to introduce contrasts
b. to sequence information   d. to introduce similarities   f. to close a presentation

____ 1. in conclusion   ____ 5. nevertheless   ____ 9. likewise
____ 2. next   ____ 6. in addition   ____ 10. yet
____ 3. similarly   ____ 7. to sum up   ____ 11. first / second / third
____ 4. to begin   ____ 8. first of all   ____ 12. furthermore

B Pair work Complete each sentence with an expression from part A. Sometimes more than one answer is possible.

(1) _____, let me thank everyone for your interest and attention as I speak on the topic of petroleum dependency – our dependency on oil for our energy needs.

There are important reasons why we should be concerned about our dependency on petroleum. (2) _____, petroleum-based fuels contribute to both air pollution and global warming, two very serious problems today. (3) _____, there is a limited supply of oil in the world; therefore, we must reduce fuel consumption and be prepared to replace petroleum with other sources of energy.

There are many ways in which to do this on a large scale. First, we must produce fuel-efficient cars; (4) _____, we must encourage the use of public transportation. Finally, tax breaks could be offered to businesses that conserve fuel. (5) _____, homeowners could also be offered tax incentives for fuel conservation. It's true that cutting down on consumption is beneficial to the environment; (6) _____, we should keep in mind that cutting down too quickly could have a negative effect on the economy.

(7) _____, this problem has no simple answers, but if the government, corporations, and private citizens all work together, I feel we can solve the problem.

VOCABULARY PLUS *see page 139*

5 LISTENING
Getting your message across

🔊 **A** Listen to advice about speaking in public. Choose the items the speaker mentions.

	Advice		Advice
☐ the audience		☐ posture	
☐ the outline		☐ eye contact	
☐ pronunciation		☐ voice	
☐ practicing		☐ questions	
☐ humor		☐ speed	

🔊 **B** Listen again. Complete the chart with the advice you hear.

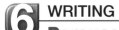

Persuasive writing

In persuasive writing, you take a position on an issue and try to convince the reader that your position is correct. To do so, you present both sides of the issue, providing arguments, reasons, and examples that support your point of view and show weaknesses of the opposing point of view.

A Read the article. What is the writer's position? What are the arguments for the opposing view? What arguments, reasons, and examples does the writer give to support his position and to show the weakness of the opposing viewpoint?

Every Student Should Be Required to Study a Foreign Language
by Leo Fernández

Recently, a student organization at our university proposed that we do away with our foreign language requirement, which mandates that all students complete two years of foreign language study. The main reason for this proposal seems to be to eliminate unnecessary courses; however, the proponents of this change are overlooking the great benefits foreign language study provides to students of any major.

Students who oppose the language requirement argue that university study should be more career focused. They feel that the language requirement steals time that could be spent on courses directly related to a student's major. This is a shortsighted position. Statistics suggest that candidates proficient in two languages have an increased chance of finding work. For example, . . .

Another point often made by the proponents of the change is that a large number of students who study a language for two years rarely use it again in their lives. While this may be true in some cases, study of a foreign language has been shown to further develop native language skills. In addition, the understanding of oneself and one's own culture is increased through contact with another language and its culture. Students who . . .

In conclusion, it is crucial that we keep the foreign language requirement. To eliminate it would be doing a great disservice to our university and its students. Foreign language learning benefits us in concrete and subtle ways as it broadens our minds and expands our opportunities.

B Pair work With a partner, take a position on one of these issues related to language, or use your own idea. Then brainstorm reasons supporting your position and weaknesses of the opposing view. Which reasons are the strongest?

- Schools should teach a second language starting in kindergarten.
- Every foreign language student should be required to study abroad.
- Institutions should be created to preserve dying languages.

C Write an article of at least four paragraphs supporting your position. Use the best reasons you have brainstormed to support your position. Make sure you argue against the opposing view.

D Pair work Exchange articles. Discuss ways the writing could be made more persuasive and the arguments stronger.

STARTING POINT
What's correct language?

A Read these statements about language. Choose the statements you agree with.

Proper English

- [ ] **1.** Most people don't need to write well. Speaking is more important.
- [ ] **2.** The majority of teenagers use too much slang.
- [ ] **3.** Three-quarters of email messages contain grammar errors.
- [ ] **4.** No one expects email to be correct.
- [ ] **5.** There are plenty of people with foreign accents who speak English well.
- [ ] **6.** None of us has the right to correct other people's grammar.
- [ ] **7.** All varieties of English are equally valid. Every variety is correct.
- [ ] **8.** A lot of advanced grammar is complicated even for native speakers.
- [ ] **9.** Only a minority of my friends cares about speaking correctly.

B Pair work Discuss your opinions with a partner.

"I disagree with the first sentence. A lot of people need to write well for their jobs."

② **DISCUSSION**
Text speak

A Pair work Read about "text speak." Then try to figure out what the six examples of text speak mean, and write the meanings. (For the answers, see page 142.)

"Text speak" refers to shortened forms of words commonly used in text messaging. When texting began, telephone companies would charge by the word, so fewer words and letters meant cheaper messages. These days, many people find text speak convenient and cool, and it is creeping into less informal types of writing. See some examples of text speak in the box.

b4	*before*
ruok?	_____
cul8r	_____
xlnt	_____
gr8	_____
2nite	_____

B Group work Read these opinions about text speak. Which one do you most agree with? Discuss your opinions about text speak with the group.

I try not to use text speak – except when I'm online or texting, of course – because it's annoying. I think people who use it in schoolwork and formal emails look idiotic and immature. — Raphael

I really feel old when my kids – and even my wife! – write to me using text speak. Nevertheless, I know that language always evolves. Just think of the difference between our English and Shakespeare's! — Rob

Txt spk is gr8! It's much easier and quicker, and u can use it for email, taking notes in class, and even in some homework assignments. — Wendy

People are free to use text speak if they think it's more convenient – after all, it's a free country. But I do hope it remains an alternative style, and that grammar is maintained. — Su-jin

③ GRAMMAR

Subject-verb agreement with quantifiers

All (of), *a lot of*, *lots of*, *plenty of*, *some (of)*, *most (of)*, and fractions take a singular verb if the noun they modify is uncountable or singular. They take a plural verb if the noun they modify is plural.
A lot of advanced **grammar is** complicated.
Most people don't need to write well.
Three-quarters of email **messages contain** grammar errors.

Each of, *every one of*, *none of*, and collective nouns, such as *majority (of)* and *minority (of)*, typically take a singular verb, but often take a plural verb after a plural noun in informal speech.
None of us has / have the right to correct other people's grammar.
The **majority of** teenagers **use / uses** too much slang.
A **minority of** my friends **care / cares** about speaking correctly.

Everyone, someone, anyone, no one, each + noun, and *every* + noun are followed by a singular verb.
Every variety **is** correct.
No one expects email to be correct.

GRAMMAR PLUS *see page 125*

A Look at the Starting Point on page 84 again. Can you find other quantifiers?
Are they followed by a singular or plural verb?

B Complete these sentences with the correct form of the verb in parentheses.
Use the simple present.

1. A lot of people ____*agree*____ (agree) that spelling and grammar shouldn't change.
2. All of the students in my class _____ (attend) English club meetings.
3. Most of the faculty at school _____ (speak) at least three languages.
4. A quarter of my classmates _____ (be) going to study abroad next semester.
5. The majority of people _____ (use) text speak in their emails.
6. None of the information in the email _____ (be) correct.
7. Every letter I receive usually _____ (contain) one or two spelling mistakes.
8. Over four-fifths of the world population _____ (be) able to read and write.

C Group work Complete these sentences with information about how people use language in different situations. Then discuss your answers.

1. Lots of the slang people use these days . . .
2. The majority of people my age . . .
3. Some of the language older people use . . .
4. None of my friends . . .
5. Most of the news anchors you see on TV . . .
6. Every one of my teachers . . .

"Lots of the slang people use these days comes from words they hear in popular music."

"That's true. In hip-hop slang, 'crib' means home, and 'bling' means flashy jewelry."

4 VOCABULARY
A way with words

A The expressions on the left can be used to comment on the way people speak. Match them with their definitions on the right.

1. have a sharp tongue ____
2. have a way with words ____
3. stick to the point ____
4. talk around a point ____
5. talk behind someone's back ____
6. talk someone into something ____
7. talk someone's ear off ____
8. love to hear oneself talk ____

a. talk about something without addressing it directly
b. enjoy talking even if nobody is paying attention
c. talk about a person without him or her knowing
d. continue talking about a main idea
e. talk in a bitter, critical way
f. talk until the other person is tired of listening
g. convince a person to do something
h. have a talent for speaking

B Pair work Use expressions from above to comment on these people and the way they are speaking.

1 | Klaus
"I wouldn't say I dislike the book, or at least I don't think so. I guess it's hard to say."

2 | Risa
"Why don't you want to go? Come on! It'll be fun, and it's cheap. I'll even drive!"

3 | Sandra
"Just be quiet! You don't know what you're talking about, so stop wasting my time!"

4 | Philip
"Diane got an F on her test. She tried to put it away quickly, but I saw it anyway!"

VOCABULARY PLUS see page 139

5 LISTENING & SPEAKING
Assert yourself!

A Listen to three one-sided conversations. Write the number of the conversation next to the correct description.

____ a. One person is talking the other person's ear off.
____ b. One person is trying to talk the other person into doing something.
____ c. One person isn't sticking to the point.

B Listen again. Which expressions do you hear used in the conversations? Write the number of the conversation next to the correct expression.

____ a. Could I say something?
____ b. Thanks for asking, but . . .
____ c. I just wanted to say . . .
____ d. That's nice, but we really need to . . .
____ e. That's really nice of you, but . . .
____ f. Getting back to what we were talking about . . .

C Pair work Prepare a conversation similar to those from the listening. Use the expressions in part B. Then perform the scene for the class.

A **Pair work** Read the quote in the first line of the article. What do you think it means? Then read the article to compare your ideas to the author's.

SLANG Abroad

George Bernard Shaw said, "England and America are two countries separated by a common language." I never really understood the meaning of this quote until a friend and I stopped at a London convenience store. We had some trash to throw away, so I, in as polite a manner as I could muster, asked the clerk for a trash can. Then I asked him again, thinking he didn't hear me. And then I asked again, only this time while speaking the international language (loudly and slowly while pointing to the object I wanted to throw away). After this horribly rude display, he politely asked me what a trash can was. So I told him it was a place for my garbage. I guess this weak explanation worked. The clerk then produced a small trash can from behind the counter and in the most you-must-not-be-from-around-here tone he could muster said, "rubbish bin."

Different names for objects, however, are not the main problem. Anyone can learn a language. But to really be a speaker of the language, you need to understand its idioms and its slang. There is a distinct difference between someone who learned a language in a classroom and someone who is a native speaker. Using slang proves that the speaker has been in a country long enough to learn it, and that offers a benefit greater than just being able to converse on a casual level. It allows the two speakers to get much closer much more quickly.

Eventually, after living somewhere for a while you pick up a few things, and this new language education gives a credibility that just pronouncing a city address cannot. It shows a belonging and membership in the club of permanent residents and that one is not just a mere extended tourist. I know it sounds superficial, that by being able to understand words that may or may not be in a dictionary, we can fool people into thinking we belong, but it isn't. What knowing and using slang shows is a basic understanding of a culture. It offers both members of the conversation a common ground.

And that's the point. Britain and America are two countries separated by a common language, but then again so are Mexico and Spain, Brazil and Portugal, and France and Haiti. While these countries' languages may all seem the same on paper, they're not. Really learning the languages can only be done on the ground. And once that learning is done, something far greater is achieved than just not sounding like a fool.

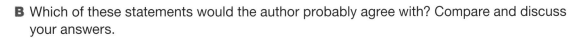

RUBBISH BIN / TRASH CAN

Source: "Slang Abroad," by Ben Falk, The Daily Colonial

B Which of these statements would the author probably agree with? Compare and discuss your answers.

1. It's impossible for anyone learning a foreign language to ever sound like a native speaker.
2. Studying books about slang is an effective way to learn how it's used.
3. Despite how connected the world is, slang and idioms remain very local.
4. Really learning a language means knowing how people actually use it.

C **Group work** Discuss these questions. Then share your answers with the class.

1. Do you agree with the author's idea that one can only really learn a language by living in a country where it's spoken? Why or why not?
2. Have you or anyone you know ever had any experiences like the one in the first paragraph? What happened? Do you think such misunderstandings are common?

11 EXCEPTIONAL PEOPLE

LESSON A ▶ *High achievers*

1 STARTING POINT
They've had an impact!

A Read about the exceptional people below. Have you heard of any of them? What sort of impact have they had on other people?

MAHATMA GANDHI

(1869–1948) Gandhi was a great political and spiritual leader in India. Although he was educated in England, Gandhi is best remembered for his struggle for Indian independence, which had far-reaching effects. His epoch-making victories through peaceful means later inspired other great leaders, like Martin Luther King Jr. and Aung San Suu Kyi.

NATALIA VODIANOVA

(1982–) Born in Russia, this blue-eyed, brown-haired beauty was working at a fruit stand by age 11. At 17, she moved to Paris and soon after signed with a well-known modeling agency. She was well received and quickly became a popular fashion model. A kind-hearted superstar, she created the Naked Heart Foundation to build playgrounds for underprivileged children in Russia.

ANDRE AGASSI

(1970–) Andre Agassi's hard-driving father always planned to make him a tennis star. Intensely coached, he was practicing with pros by age five. During his career, Agassi won every important tournament at least once and earned over 100 million dollars. Now retired but socially engaged, he built a free school for youth in one of Las Vegas's poorest neighborhoods.

B **Group work** Think of people who have had an impact on the world. Discuss their achievements, and then choose the person who has had the biggest impact.

2 DISCUSSION
Exceptional values

A **Group work** Think about the people you talked about in the Starting Point. What values do you think were most important to each of them? Why?

"I think Gandhi valued patience. He had patience with people and patience to achieve his goal through nonviolent measures."

B Look at this list of life values. Choose the three that are the most important in your life. If your top values aren't here, add them to the list.

- ☐ achievement
- ☐ compassion
- ☐ cooperation
- ☐ creativity
- ☐ environmentalism
- ☐ health
- ☐ independence
- ☐ responsibility
- ☐ spirituality
- ☐ wealth
- ☐ _____
- ☐ _____

C **Group work** Explain your choices to the members of your group. Then make a list of the three life values that are the most important to your group as a whole.

3 GRAMMAR

Compound adjectives

Compound adjectives are modifying phrases made up of two or more words. They can be joined by a hyphen, appear as a single word, or appear as two separate words. Always check a dictionary before using compound adjectives in writing.

Three common patterns for compound adjectives in English are:

a. adjective + noun + -ed *(absent-minded, high-spirited, long-winded, soft-hearted)*
When preceding a noun, these compounds are usually written with a hyphen unless they are one word.

b. adverb + past participle *(much-loved, well-dressed, highly acclaimed, widely respected)*
Compounds with adverbs ending in *-ly* are never hyphenated.
Other adverbs are usually hyphenated before but not after the noun.

c. adjective, adverb, or noun + present participle *(easygoing, forward-thinking, thought-provoking)*
When preceding a noun, these compounds are usually written with a hyphen unless they are one word.

GRAMMAR PLUS *see page 126*

A Look at the Starting Point on page 88 again. Can you find more compound adjectives? Which patterns from the grammar box do they follow?

B Rewrite these sentences using the compound adjectives from the Starting Point to replace the words in boldface. Sometimes more than one answer is possible.

1. Roger Federer is an athlete **everybody knows**.
   Roger Federer is a well-known athlete.

2. The play was **praised** by most theater critics.

3. Many charities are set up to help children **who are poor**.

4. The **very generous** celebrity gave money to the homeless.

5. The work of Gandhi had effects **that reached around the world**.

6. The child **with blue eyes** was adopted by a celebrity.

4 VOCABULARY

Compound adjectives related to the body

A Combine the words from both boxes to create compound adjectives and match them with their synonyms below. Sometimes more than one answer is possible.

absent	cool	hard	narrow	soft	blooded	hearted
cold	empty	hot	open	warm	headed	minded

1. silly and brainless *empty-headed*
2. quick to anger _____
3. uncaring or unkind _____
4. sweet and loving _____
5. stubborn and unyielding _____

6. tolerant and unbiased _____
7. intolerant and disapproving _____
8. forgetful _____
9. calm and unexcitable _____
10. friendly and kind _____

B Pair work Use the compound adjectives in part A and others you can create to describe exceptional people or characters from movies, television, or books.

"Sherlock Holmes is an open-minded detective who uses his powers of observation to catch cold-blooded killers."

VOCABULARY PLUS *see page 140*

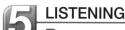

5 LISTENING
Do you want to be a high achiever?

A Listen to a speaker talk about the qualities of high achievers. Choose the four qualities he talks about.

	Suggestion		Suggestion
☐ lifelong learning		☐ positive attitude	
☐ high self-esteem		☐ risk-taking	
☐ responsibility		☐ creativity	

B Listen again. What does the speaker suggest people do in order to build the four qualities of high achievers? Write the suggestions in the chart.

6 DISCUSSION
Winning words

A **Pair work** Read these quotations from high achievers. Can you restate these quotations in your own words?

a

Mark Zuckerberg
entrepreneur
"The biggest risk is not taking any risk."

d

Andrea Jung
businesswoman
"If you feel like it's difficult to change, you will probably have a harder time succeeding."

b

Gloria Estefan
singer
"You don't have to give up who you are to be successful just because you're different."

e

Laird Hamilton
surfer and model
"Make sure your worst enemy doesn't live between your own two ears."

c

Donald Trump
businessman and TV personality
"If you're going to be thinking anyway, you might as well think big!"

Useful expressions

Describing what something means

What this means to me is that . . .
My understanding of this is that . . .
I interpret this to mean . . .

B **Group work** Which of the quotations in part A might be useful for the following kinds of people? Do you know any other sayings or quotations that might be helpful?

1. someone who wants to get rich in business
2. someone who wants success but worries about how much work or time it will take
3. someone who wants to study abroad but is afraid of not fitting in somewhere new
4. someone who is only working part-time and putting off starting a real career
5. someone who is hesitant to register for a class because of self-doubt

WRITING
Biographical profile

A biographical profile usually begins with an introduction that includes a thesis statement about what makes the person interesting or special. The subsequent paragraphs are then usually arranged in chronological order.

A The paragraphs in this biographical profile about J. K. Rowling have been scrambled. Read the composition and put the paragraphs in order.

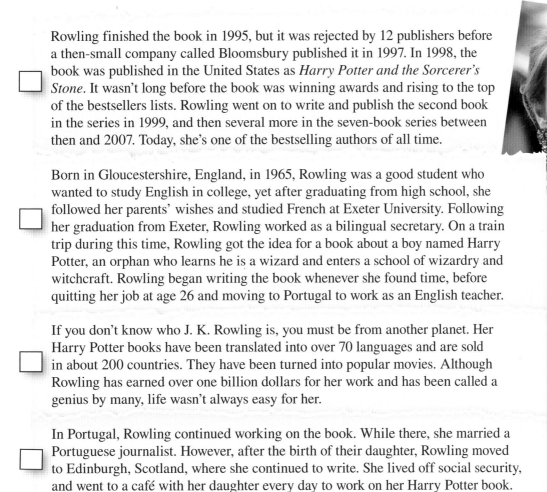

☐ Rowling finished the book in 1995, but it was rejected by 12 publishers before a then-small company called Bloomsbury published it in 1997. In 1998, the book was published in the United States as *Harry Potter and the Sorcerer's Stone*. It wasn't long before the book was winning awards and rising to the top of the bestsellers lists. Rowling went on to write and publish the second book in the series in 1999, and then several more in the seven-book series between then and 2007. Today, she's one of the bestselling authors of all time.

☐ Born in Gloucestershire, England, in 1965, Rowling was a good student who wanted to study English in college, yet after graduating from high school, she followed her parents' wishes and studied French at Exeter University. Following her graduation from Exeter, Rowling worked as a bilingual secretary. On a train trip during this time, Rowling got the idea for a book about a boy named Harry Potter, an orphan who learns he is a wizard and enters a school of wizardry and witchcraft. Rowling began writing the book whenever she found time, before quitting her job at age 26 and moving to Portugal to work as an English teacher.

☐ If you don't know who J. K. Rowling is, you must be from another planet. Her Harry Potter books have been translated into over 70 languages and are sold in about 200 countries. They have been turned into popular movies. Although Rowling has earned over one billion dollars for her work and has been called a genius by many, life wasn't always easy for her.

☐ In Portugal, Rowling continued working on the book. While there, she married a Portuguese journalist. However, after the birth of their daughter, Rowling moved to Edinburgh, Scotland, where she continued to write. She lived off social security, and went to a café with her daughter every day to work on her Harry Potter book.

B Choose a famous person you know a lot about. Make notes and list key events from this person's life in chronological order. Then use your notes to write a biographical profile.

C **Pair work** Exchange profiles with a partner, and answer these questions.

1. Does your partner's profile begin with an introduction and include a thesis statement?
2. Is the information in the profile arranged in chronological order?
3. Can you suggest any improvements to make the profile more interesting or effective?
4. What else would you like to know about the person your partner wrote about?

LESSON B ▶ *People we admire*

1 STARTING POINT
Role models

A Read these online posts about role models. What life values are reflected in each post?

 YOUR SPACE TO SHARE FEELINGS AND IDEAS
Up for Discussion: **Tell us about the people you respect and admire.** + new post

 RobertD They may not be the smartest or the best-looking people in the world, but I'd say my friends are the people I most admire. We stick together and watch out for each other – and learn a lot from each other, too.

 Alena92 I've always looked up to my father. He's the hardest-working and the least narrow-minded man I know. He's always taught me that hard work is the surest way to be successful.

 OwnDrummer I'm not sure I have a role model. I mostly like to do my own thing. I think it's because I'm not the most easily impressed person when I meet someone new, and I'm pretty slow to trust people.

 Sporty_girl One person I really respect is my soccer coach. He's a tough competitor, and he's the best-trained soccer player I know. He's also one of the most warm-hearted.

 Thoughtful2 My philosophy professor is my role model, definitely. Her class is the most thought-provoking one I've ever attended. Someday, I'd like to be as well respected as she is.

 Amber334 I've always wanted to be more like my sister Tonya. While I tend to worry a lot, Tonya is the most easygoing person in our family. She never lets little problems bother her.

B **Pair work** Tell your partner about someone you consider a role model. Explain why you respect and admire that person. Your partner will then tell the class about the person.

"Bruno has an enormous amount of respect for his grandfather. He started his own business when he was 18 years old . . ."

2 LISTENING
People who make a difference

 A Listen to Luisa talk about her grandmother and Chu Lan talk about his tennis coach. How do Luisa and Chu Lan feel about the people they are describing?

B Listen again. In what ways did these people influence Luisa and Chu Lan? Write two ways for each.

	How did Luisa's grandmother influence her?	How did Chu Lan's coach influence him?
1.		
2.		

3 GRAMMAR

Superlative compound adjectives

Superlative compound adjectives generally follow the same hyphenation rules
as compound adjectives.

The superlative form of compound adjectives is most often formed by adding
the most and *the least*. There is never a hyphen after *most* or *least*.
I'm not **the most easily impressed** person.
Tonya is **the most easygoing** person in our family.
He's **the least narrow-minded** man I know.

When the first word of a compound adjective is an adjective or adverb of one or
sometimes two syllables, the superlative can also be formed by adding
the and using the superlative form of the first word.
He is **the hardest-working** man I know.
They may not be the smartest or **the best-looking** people in the world.

Compound adjectives in their superlative form can also occur after the verb *be* without a noun.
Of all the men I know, he's **the hardest working**.

GRAMMAR PLUS *see page 127*

A Look at the Starting Point on page 92 again. How many superlative compound
adjectives can you find?

B Rewrite these phrases using the superlative form of the compound adjective.

1. an awe-inspiring place
   the most awe-inspiring place
2. a widely read book
3. a good-looking man
4. a thirst-quenching beverage
5. a highly developed mind
6. a warm-hearted friend
7. a far-reaching plan
8. a thought-provoking novel
9. a well-defined project
10. a bad-intentioned person

C Complete these sentences with
the superlative compound adjectives you wrote
in part B and your own ideas. Share your answers with a partner.

1. . . . natural place I've ever been to is . . .
   The most awe-inspiring natural place I've ever been to is the Grand Canyon.
2. . . . magazine in the country is probably . . .
3. In my opinion, . . . actor / actress in the world is . . .
4. On a hot day, . . . drink is . . .
5. . . . movie I've ever seen is . . .
6. . . . person I know is . . .
7. . . . leader my country has ever had is / was . . .

4 VOCABULARY
Phrasal verbs

A Read the sentences below. Then match the phrasal verbs in boldface with their definitions.

a. take care of   e. confront
b. defend or support   f. overcome
c. go see if someone is all right   g. resemble (an older relative) in looks or character
d. rely on   h. achieve what is expected

____ 1. It's only natural for children to **look to** their parents for advice.

____ 2. Sometimes we need to **get through** difficulties in order to succeed.

____ 3. Before parents go to bed, they should **check on** their kids and see if they're OK.

____ 4. I expect my children to **look after** me when I reach old age.

____ 5. Parents need to teach their children to **face up to** their problems and solve them.

____ 6. When I argue with my sister, it seems like my parents **side with** her.

____ 7. The children of accomplished parents often find it difficult to **live up to** the high expectations people have for them.

____ 8. When it comes to finances, I **take after** my dad; he could never save money either.

B **Pair work** Discuss the sentences in part A with a partner. Comment on the statements, and talk about how they apply to your life.

"I find that the older I get, the more I look to my parents for advice."

VOCABULARY PLUS *see page 140*

5 DISCUSSION
Everyday heroism

A **Pair work** Read what Farah says about heroic behavior. What is her definition of a hero? Do you agree with the definition? Do you have other examples?

To me, heroes often aren't the most widely recognized people, and on the surface, their actions don't necessarily seem to be the most awe inspiring. A hero could be a parent who, after an exhausting day, helps a child with a difficult homework assignment. It could be a person on the street who picks up and returns something you didn't realize you'd dropped, someone who stops by to check on you when you're ill, someone who sides with you when you've been wronged, or someone who takes time out of a busy schedule to help you with a problem. A hero is not just a person who has the courage to take a risk; he or she is also a person who has the courage to always be kind to people no matter what they're going through.

Farah, 26

B **Group work** Discuss these situations. What would you do to make a difference?

a *Your next-door neighbor fell and broke her leg. She lives by herself.*

b The condition of your neighborhood park has deteriorated, and fewer and fewer people are using it.

c Children in a nearby low-income neighborhood seem to have few opportunities for academic success.

d A friend of yours has lost his or her job and can't seem to find another one.

"I would check on my neighbor from time to time and help her with some of her daily chores."

A Pair work Do you know any nongovernmental organizations (NGOs)? Discuss some of the ways they are making a change. Then read the article.

ANN COTTON, *SOCIAL ENTREPRENEUR*

The following is an interview with Ann Cotton, founder and chief executive of the Campaign for Female Education (Camfed), an NGO whose programs invest in the education of girls and young women and have benefited over two million children in the poorest areas of Africa.

How do you define a social entrepreneur? Someone who witnesses the pain and struggle in the lives of others and is compelled to act and to work with them.

What skills are needed to be a social entrepreneur? You need to be absolutely dogged. You need to listen to the people experiencing the problems, and their ideas need to crowd out the words of the "can't be done-ers."

How did your work as a former teacher and head of children's assessment help in setting up Camfed? There will always be children who don't fit the institution and whose sense of exclusion is reinforced day by day. Their experience shaped my approach to children and young people in Africa.

How did you learn how to run a successful charity? I learned by doing, and from others who were encouraging and generous in their help. I belonged to a community of activists that was inspirational.

How did you manage the growth of Camfed from supporting 32 girls, with £2,000 raised from selling your homemade cakes, to a £3,000,000 NGO? Lucy Lake [currently chief executive officer] and I built the whole model from the grassroots up. Donors could see it was working and began to get behind us in increasing numbers. We attract and retain outstanding individuals. In Africa, the early beneficiaries head the programs – young women who share a background of rural poverty, transformation through education, and the courage to bring about change.

What has been the key to the success of Camfed? Never take your eye off the ball. Always remember that you and everyone on the team are the servant of the cause – in our case, girls' education and young women's leadership in Africa.

What advice would you give tomorrow's social entrepreneurs? Be greedy for social change, and your life will be endlessly enriched. The only failure lies in not trying, or giving up.

What is the best piece of management advice you have received? Have faith in your intuition and listen to your gut feeling.

Source: "Leading Questions," interview by Alison Benjamin, *The Guardian*

B Are these statements about the reading true (*T*), false (*F*), or is the information not given (*NG*) in the interview? Write the correct letters.

_____ 1. According to Ann Cotton, a social entrepreneur feels driven to help those who suffer in life.

_____ 2. Ann Cotton's experience of being excluded in school has guided her approach to setting up Camfed.

_____ 3. Today, Camfed continues to fund its programs through cake sales.

_____ 4. Camfed's programs are run only by the most highly trained experts in management.

_____ 5. Camfed's cause is to educate young women in Africa and encourage them to become leaders.

_____ 6. Ann Cotton thinks managers should trust their instincts.

C Group work Discuss these questions with your group.

1. How does Ann Cotton explain the success of Camfed? Which of the factors mentioned do you think were the most important?

2. Do you think Ann Cotton is an exceptional individual, or could anyone have done what she did? Explain your answer.

12 BUSINESS MATTERS

LESSON A ▶ *Entrepreneurs*

1 STARTING POINT
Success stories

A Match these descriptions of successful companies with the company name.

_____ 1. The Body Shop   _____ 2. Google   _____ 3. Sanrio

a. Larry Page and **Sergey Brin** started this innovative company in a dorm room at Stanford University. They didn't get along at first, and had they been unable to work together, the most widely used Internet search engine might never have been created. Should you ask about their company's goal, they'll probably smile and tell you it's to organize all of the world's information in order to make it accessible and useful.

b. Should you want to buy natural skin and hair care products, this company offers over 1,200 choices. **Anita Roddick** started the company to support her family. Had she been wealthy, she might not have gone into business. These stores communicate a message about human rights and environmental issues. The company is famous for its fair trade practices in impoverished communities.

c. In 1960, **Shintaro Tsuji** created a line of character-branded lifestyle products centered around gift-giving occasions. However, had this Tokyo-based company not created Hello Kitty, it wouldn't have become nearly so successful. Hello Kitty goods are in demand all over the world. They include purses, wastebaskets, pads and pens, erasers, cell phone holders, and much, much more.

B Pair work Discuss these questions.

1. What might be some reasons for the success of these companies?
2. Can you think of other successful companies? What do they offer?

2 LISTENING
Unsuccessful endeavors

A Group work Brainstorm some of the factors that can make a new business fail.

🔊 **B** Listen to two people discuss their unsuccessful attempts to start a business. What types of business did they try to get into? Why did they choose those types? Complete the chart.

	Type of business	Reason for choosing it
1.		
2.		

🔊 **C** Listen again. Write the main reasons why each attempt failed.

1. _____
2. _____

3 GRAMMAR

Subject-verb inversion in conditional sentences

In past unreal conditional sentences, people sometimes replace *if* by inverting the subject and the auxiliary *had*. This occurs mainly in more formal speech and writing.

If they **had been** unable to work together, the search engine **might never have been** created.
Had they **been** unable to work together, the search engine **might never have been** created.

The same construction is possible for negative sentences. Notice that negative forms are not contracted and *not* is separated from *had* in these sentences.

If this company **hadn't created** Hello Kitty, it **wouldn't have become** nearly so successful.
Had this company **not created** Hello Kitty, it **wouldn't have become** nearly so successful.

In present and future real conditionals, people often replace *if* by putting *should* at the beginning of the sentence. Note that this use of *should* does not express obligation.

If you **want** to buy natural skin care products, this company offers over 1,200 choices.
Should you **want** to buy natural skin care products, this company offers over 1,200 choices.

GRAMMAR PLUS *see page 128*

A Look at the Starting Point on page 96 again. Can you find other conditional sentences with subject-verb inversion?

B Combine these pairs of sentences using conditional clauses and subject-verb inversion. Then compare with a partner. Sometimes more than one answer is possible.

1. That company didn't take the competition into consideration. It went out of business.
   Had that company taken the competition into consideration, it wouldn't have gone out of business.

2. That fast-food chain hasn't offered any healthy food options. Its sales are down.

3. Terry didn't develop a serious business plan. She missed a number of opportunities.

4. I decided to go to business school. I started my own business.

5. The government doesn't encourage international business. The economy is slowing down.

6. My friends and I didn't know enough about the potential of the Internet. We didn't start an online business.

7. I knew it would take 10 years to pay off my college loans. I chose an affordable school.

8. I thought my friend's business idea would fail. I didn't lend her any money.

C **Pair work** Complete these sentences with your own information, and share them with a partner.

1. Had I saved more money when I was younger, . . .

2. Should all the students in the class start a small business, . . .

3. Had I not decided to take this English course, . . .

4. Had I followed my parents' advice, I would have . . .

5. Should I have the opportunity to start a business, I might . . .

6. Had I known five years ago what I know now, I'd probably . . .

4 VOCABULARY
Prepositions following *work*

A The expressions on the left are composed of *work* and a preposition.
Match them with their definitions on the right.

1. work **against** your interests ____
2. work **around** a problem ____
3. work **for** a boss ____
4. work **toward** a goal ____
5. work **off** a debt ____
6. work **on** a task ____

a. be employed by
b. apply effort to
c. make it harder (for someone) to achieve something
d. work while avoiding (a difficulty)
e. work in order to achieve
f. work in order to eliminate

B Complete each statement with the correct preposition.

1. Entrepreneurs don't waste time trying to solve insolvable problems; they work _____ them.

2. Inexperience can work _____ young people looking for jobs.

3. Workers are happier when they work _____ a variety of projects, not just the same one.

4. My uncle lent me $4,000 to buy a car, but he's letting me work _____ part of the loan by painting his house.

> **VOCABULARY PLUS** *see page 141*

5 DISCUSSION
Too good to be true?

A Read these advertising messages for different job opportunities. Which do you find the most believable? Which do you find the least? Why?

❶ Break into the fashion industry! Our classes are your first step to working toward your goal of becoming a glamorous fashion model.

❷ Start your career in real estate. You can buy houses for as little as $2,000 and resell them for a huge profit with our real-estate buying program.

> **Useful expressions**
>
> **Expressing suspicion**
> That's a little hard to believe.
> It sounds fishy to me.
> It sounds too good to be true.

❸ Get paid for your time on social networking sites. Earn thousands every month just for posting comments!

❹ How would you like to get paid just for going shopping? Does it sound too good to be true? It's not. Ask us how!

❺ Invest like a professional. Send us $50 for information on how to make millions in the stock market.

"In my opinion, the most believable one is number three. I read that companies pay people to write positive posts about their products. The one I found hardest to believe is . . ."

B Group work Discuss the questions with your group.

1. What would probably happen if you replied to an ad like one of those above?
2. What are some other examples of hard-to-believe advertisements?
3. Who do you think is attracted to these types of messages? Why?

> Formal letters don't include personal information that is irrelevant to the topic. Unlike personal letters, formal letters tend to avoid contractions and idioms.

A Read this formal letter. Then label the five parts listed in the box.

1 The **heading** includes your address and the date. It typically goes in the top left corner. If you use letterhead stationery with an address, only the date is added.

2 The **inside address** is below the heading. It contains the addressee's name, title (if you know it), and address.

3 For the **greeting**, you should write "Dear" and "Mr." or "Ms." along with the person's family name. If you don't have a specific person to contact, write "Dear Sir or Madam." The greeting is usually followed by a colon (:).

4 The **body** of the letter follows. The first paragraph is used to state the reason for the letter. The paragraphs that follow should each focus on only one point. The letter generally concludes by thanking the reader in some way.

5 The **closing** includes a closing phrase, your signature, and your name and title (if you have one).

1 —

335 Henry St.
New York, NY 10002

July 10, 2014

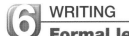

DM
DONNA MALNICK

Mr. Jonathan Hayes, Director
Institute for Study Abroad
1472 Park Avenue
Summit, NJ 07091

Dear Mr. Hayes:

I am writing to request more information concerning your study abroad programs. Your programs sound extremely interesting, and I hope to participate in one of them next year. Your Study Abroad in Paris program sounds particularly fascinating.

I would like to sign up for the Paris program beginning in June. I'm still trying to decide whether to choose the homestay option or the dormitory option. Would it be possible to send me further information about those two choices in order to help me make a decision?

I realize that all the spaces in your Paris program may already be filled. In that case, my second choice would be the Study Abroad in Toulouse program. My third choice would be your Study Abroad in Strasbourg program.

Thank you very much for your help. I look forward to receiving the information.

Sincerely,

Donna Malnick
Donna Malnick

B Imagine that you are interested in learning more about a study program. Write your formal letter to the program director expressing interest and requesting information. Include all five parts of a formal letter.

STARTING POINT

Attitudes at work

A What kinds of working conditions would you like at your job? Choose the statements you agree with.

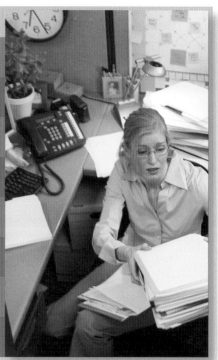

What are you **looking for** in a JOB?

1 I would be happier and more productive if my workspace were neat and organized.

2 I would take almost any job provided that there were opportunities to learn.

3 I wouldn't care about a high salary if a job allowed me to balance my work, family, and social life.

4 I wouldn't mind working in an office, assuming that I had the freedom to be creative.

5 If the company I worked for dealt fairly with me, I would be loyal to it.

6 I would only take a job on the condition that it offered long-term security.

7 I would quit a job that required me to be dishonest, whether or not it were high paying.

8 Supposing I had the choice, I would prefer to work with a group rather than by myself.

B Group work Compare your answers with the members of your group. How are you different? Do you think you would make a harmonious group of co-workers?

 DISCUSSION

The dream job

A Look at this checklist of considerations in choosing a job. Add two more items to the list. Then choose the three items that are the most important to you.

The ideal job . . .

☐ allows me to travel often.

☐ offers me a high salary.

☐ isn't stressful at all.

☐ doesn't require long hours.

☐ gives me the freedom to be creative.

☐ has a flexible schedule.

☐ lets me wear casual clothes.

☐ has an excellent health plan and benefits.

☐ has lots of opportunity for advancement.

☐ is close to my home or school.

☐ _____.

☐ _____.

B Pair work Share your ideas with a partner. Explain and compare your choices.

"For me, the ideal job should have a flexible schedule so that I always have time for family and a social life . . ."

3 GRAMMAR

Adverb clauses of condition

Conditional sentences do not necessarily use *if*. The following expressions are also used.
The tense agreement in the clauses is the same as in conditional sentences with *if*.

Provided (*that*) and *on the condition* (*that*) introduce a condition on which another situation depends.
I would take almost any job **provided that** there were opportunities to learn.
I would only take a job **on the condition that** it offered long-term security.

Whether or not introduces a condition that does not influence another situation.
I would quit a job that required me to be dishonest, **whether or not** it were high paying.

Assuming (*that*) introduces an assumption upon which another condition depends.
I wouldn't mind working in an office, **assuming that** I had the freedom to be creative.

Supposing (*that*) introduces a possible condition that could influence another situation.
Supposing I had the choice, I would prefer to work with a group rather than by myself.

GRAMMAR PLUS *see page 129*

A Look at the Starting Point on page 100 again. Can you replace the sentences with *if* with another expression?

B Match the items to make logical sentences.

1. Whether or not you have a clear job description, ____
2. Assuming that you have an original idea, ____
3. On the condition that I didn't have to be away for more than two or three days, ____
4. Provided that I could find extra time, ____
5. Supposing a close friend wanted to start a business with you, ____
6. Whether or not I actually get the job, ____

a. you might be able to start a successful business.
b. I would be willing to travel on business.
c. would you jump at the opportunity?
d. I felt the interview process was a valuable experience.
e. you need to be flexible and cooperative.
f. I'd like to do some volunteer work.

C **Pair work** Complete these sentences with your own information. Then discuss them with a partner.

1. I would enjoy managing an office, assuming . . .
   I had responsible people working for me.
2. Provided a company paid for my commute, I . . .
3. Whether or not I have enough money in the bank, I . . .
4. I would take a reduction in salary on the condition that . . .
5. Supposing that I couldn't find a job, I . . .
6. I would agree to work overtime, assuming that . . .
7. On the condition that I were guaranteed two weeks' vacation a year, . . .

4 VOCABULARY & SPEAKING
Qualities essential for success

A Choose three qualities that are important to working alone successfully and three that are important to working well with others. Write them in the chart.

A **SUCCESSFUL** WORKER NEEDS TO . . . .

have good communication skills

have initiative

be trustworthy

have leadership ability

have influence

have charisma

have self-discipline

be innovative

be adaptable

be optimistic

be conscientious

have specialized training

To work alone successfully, you need to	To work well with others, you need to . . . .
have initiative	

B Pair work Discuss the qualities you chose. Why do you think they're important?

"I feel you can work alone successfully, provided you have initiative."

"I totally agree. You need to have a lot of initiative because you don't have a boss to tell you what to do."

VOCABULARY PLUS *see page 141*

5 LISTENING
Can you really learn that?

◀)) **A** Listen to three people who participated in workshops for their jobs. What type of workshop did each person attend?

1. Anne: _____ 2. Thomas: _____ 3. Paulina: _____

◀)) **B** Listen again. What did each person learn from his or her workshop experience?

Anne: _____

Thomas: _____

Paulina: _____

C Pair work Would you like to take part in such workshops? Why or why not? Discuss your reasons.

READING
Working with others

A Pair work Do your friends tend to have similar values and temperaments?
Read the article and make a list of three categories that your friends would fit into.

THE VALUE OF
DIFFERENCE

Every person is unique. We work with many people who are different from us. It is important to realize that differences are good and to appreciate that not all people are like us. On a team, the strengths of one worker can overcome the weaknesses of another. The balance created by such variety makes a team stronger.

There are three basic ways that people differ from one another: values, temperament, and individual diversity (gender, age, etc.).

Values are the importance that we give to ideas, things, or people. While our values may be quite different, organizational behavior expert Stephen Robbins suggests that people fall into one of three general categories:

Traditionalists: People in this category value hard work, doing things the way they've always been done, loyalty to the organization, and the authority of leaders.

Humanists: People in this category value quality of life, autonomy, loyalty to self, and leaders who are attentive to workers' needs.

Pragmatists: People in this category value success, achievement, loyalty to career, and leaders who reward people for hard work.

Another important way in which people differ is temperament. Your temperament is the distinctive way you think, feel, and react to the world. All of us have our own individual temperament. However, experts have found that it is easier to understand the differences in temperament by classifying people into four categories:

Optimists: People with this temperament must be free and not tied down. They're impulsive, they enjoy the immediate, and they like working with things. The optimist is generous and cheerful and enjoys action for action's sake.

Realists: People with this temperament like to belong to groups. They have a strong sense of obligation and are committed to society's standards. The realist is serious, likes order, and finds traditions important.

Futurists: People with this temperament like to control things and are also self-critical. They strive for excellence and live for work. The futurist focuses on the future and is highly creative.

Idealists: People with this temperament want to know the meaning of things. They appreciate others and get along well with people of all temperaments. The idealist is romantic, writes fluently, and values integrity.

Source: Job Savvy: How to Be a Success at Work, by LaVerne Ludden

B Match the categories from the article with the descriptions.

1. traditionalist _____
2. humanist _____
3. pragmatist _____
4. optimist _____
5. realist _____
6. futurist _____
7. idealist _____

a. generous and cheerful; enjoys action for action's sake
b. serious and likes order; has a strong sense of obligation
c. values quality of life; attentive to workers' needs
d. strives for excellence; focuses on the future
e. values doing things the way they've always been done
f. romantic; writes fluently; values integrity
g. values loyalty to career, success, and achievement

C Group work Discuss these questions. Then share your answers with the class.

1. How would you categorize your own values and temperament? Give examples.
2. Which category of people would you prefer to work with on a challenging project? Explain.

COMMUNICATION REVIEW

✓ SELF-ASSESSMENT

How well can you do these things? Choose the best answer.

I can . . .	Very well	OK	A little
▸ Take part in a discussion about what people have to do to succeed in difficult situations (Ex. 1)	☐	☐	☐
▸ Understand a lecture about language learning (Ex. 2)	☐	☐	☐
▸ Describe people's personal qualities and give reasons for my descriptions (Ex. 3)	☐	☐	☐
▸ Describe and evaluate my own personal qualities (Ex. 4)	☐	☐	☐

Now do the corresponding exercises. Was your assessment correct?

1 SPEAKING
Speaking tips

A Pair work What would each person have to do to succeed? Think of several conditions that would work for each situation.

1. Mary has been asked to give a formal talk on a topic she knows little about.
2. Julia has been asked to give a short speech at a friend's wedding.
3. Hal is too timid to join in the group's conversation after class.
4. Tom had some bad experiences at job interviews, and now he gets really nervous before them.

B Group work Discuss your ideas with another pair. Do you have similar suggestions?

"Providing Mary spends time reading about the topic, she shouldn't have a problem."
"That's true, assuming she has time to do plenty of research and rehearse first."

2 LISTENING
Good language learners

 A Listen to a lecture about good language learning. Who is the lecture for? Choose the correct answer.

☐ a. people who are learning another language
☐ b. people who are going to travel abroad
☐ c. people who want to be language teachers

B Listen again. Choose the compound adjectives that are used to describe good language learners.

☐ 1. highly motivated   ☐ 4. pattern-seeking   ☐ 7. well-known
☐ 2. forward-thinking   ☐ 5. open-minded   ☐ 8. self-aware
☐ 3. risk-taking   ☐ 6. well-organized   ☐ 9. widely recognized

3 DISCUSSION
The most and the best

A Complete the sentences with your own information. Add reasons for your opinions, and compare with a partner.

1. One of the most open-minded people in my family is . . .
2. I imagine that a lot of the most hardworking people . . .
3. The most forward-thinking person I've ever met is . . .
4. The majority of my friends would agree that the best-dressed celebrities include . . .
5. The most easygoing person I've ever known is . . .
6. Some of the most well-informed people I can think of are . . .

"One of the most open-minded people in my family is my uncle John. He's always willing to go to new places and try new things."

B Pair work Who are some people you both admire? Use the superlative form of these compound adjectives to write sentences about them. Give reasons.

1. good-looking   2. thought-provoking   3. widely respected   4. kind-hearted

4 SPEAKING
Personal qualities

A Which of these people is most similar to you, and which is least similar?

Rita

"I've been told that I'm a charismatic person. The truth is that I'm a people person, and I'm not afraid to share my ideas with others."

Su Lyn

"I'm very optimistic. I try to look at the good side of things, and I'm always confident that even the worst situations will turn out to be fine."

Alberto

"I've lived in three different countries and have attended six different schools. Yet I've never had problems adapting to new situations."

B Pair work Which of these are your strongest qualities? Which do you feel are most necessary to realize your own personal and professional goals?

- adaptability
- charisma
- conscientiousness
- determination
- honesty
- initiative
- optimism
- self-confidence
- self-control

"I think I'm very adaptable. Since I'd like to be an actor, and the work is unpredictable, I think that's an important quality."

GRAMMAR PLUS

7A Optional and required relative pronouns

When the relative pronoun is the complement (or object) of a preposition, *whom* is required (not *who*).
No one can live on that land now except indigenous people **to whom** special permits have been given.

Similarly, *which* is required (not *that*) when the preposition precedes the relative pronoun.
My parents' generation stood for certain principles **against which** my generation has rebelled.

The relative pronoun *whose* is not only used for people. It can also represent animals or things. This relative pronoun is required.
There are some new fitness classes **whose** purpose is to provide safe exercise for the elderly.

1 Complete the sentences with *whom*, *which*, or *whose*.

1. Junk food advertisements are particularly effective in influencing the buying patterns of the young people to _____*whom*_____ they are aimed.

2. "Where is society heading?" is a difficult question, the answer to _____ I don't think anybody really knows.

3. That insurance company currently offers low-cost health plans to people _____ workplace doesn't offer any.

4. I'd like to join the debate about the future of international travel, but I'm afraid it's a subject about _____ I know almost nothing.

5. Improper or insufficient education is the root of intolerance. The world would change for the better if we understood the people against _____ we have prejudices.

6. My parents owned a fully detached house with a big yard. Unfortunately, my friends and I are all apartment dwellers for _____ owning such a house just isn't possible.

2 Review the rules for pronouns on page 55. Complete the text with the appropriate relative pronouns. Sometimes more than one answer is possible.

I once read a story about a little boy (1) _____*who / that*_____ received an insect – a large beetle – for his birthday. Frustrated by the insect's frantic movements, the boy turned it over and over looking for a switch (2) _____ could turn it off. Clearly, this was a boy (3) _____ understanding of animals and the natural world was extremely limited. The result was a boy for (4) _____ a living thing was indistinguishable from a toy.

Parents should expose their children to nature from a young age. There is a farm not far from the city to (5) _____ hundreds of families go every weekend. There, city kids (6) _____ might not otherwise have had the chance are able to see, and even to touch, a wide variety of living things. By encountering animals (7) _____ are real, not just pictures, children learn the important lesson that these are living creatures (8) _____ are worthy of respect, just like us.

7B As if, as though, as, the way, and like

When *as* introduces a clause expressing a comparison, subject-verb inversion can occur in affirmative sentences.
With *do*: Marissa has a lot of trouble accepting change, **as does Trina**.
With auxiliary verbs: Mitt has coped well with changes at work, **as have his co-workers**.
With modals: Grandma would tell us stories of the old days, **as would Grandpa**.
With *be*: Marcel is wary of technology, **as is his whole family**.

When both clauses have the same subject, *as if* and *as though* clauses with adjectives or past participles are frequently shortened by removing the subject and *be*.
Bill is talking about quitting his job, **as though (he were)** single and carefree.
Marvin sat motionless in front of his new media center, **as if (he were)** glued to the chair.

Notice that we use a past form of a verb after *as if* and *as though* when these phrases are followed by a hypothetical or unreal situation.
Bill is talking about quitting his job **as though** he **were** carefree. *(He has responsibilities.)*
Some young people replace their gadgets every year **as if** they **had** all the money in the world.

1 Combine these sentences using a clause expressing comparison with *as*.
Use subject-verb inversion.

1. The students at my new school welcomed me warmly. The teachers welcomed me, too.
The students at my new school welcomed me warmly, as did the teachers.

2. Moving to Spain will bring about many changes in my life. Getting a new job will, too.

3. Clarissa is enjoying retirement. Her husband is also enjoying it.

4. Claudia went to a traditional Chinese opera last night. Jim went, too.

5. The teachers' union is supporting a four-day workweek. The transit workers' union is supporting this as well.

6. I've given up my car and am taking public transportation now. Several of my co-workers are taking public transportation, too.

7. I can cope well with changes. My wife can cope well with changes, too.

8. Amber believes that it is often foolish to resist change. Josh also believes that it is often foolish to do so.

2 Rewrite the sentences, shortening the longer clauses and lengthening the shorter clauses. Follow the model in the grammar box.

1. Guests in the theater felt a strange sensation, as if transported back in time.
Guests in the theater felt a strange sensation, as if they had been transported back in time.

2. That family lives without electricity, as though they were trapped in the 1800s.

3. The music sounded great on my new sound system, as if it were played by a live band.

4. That kid's clothes looked too big for him, as though borrowed from an older brother.

5. My grandmother looks odd in that photo, as if she were annoyed.

The following verbs are commonly used with both a direct and indirect object.

bring   hand   order   pay   serve
give   make   owe   promise   throw

When the direct object is a pronoun, it goes before the indirect object.
When the indirect object is a pronoun, it can go before or after the direct object.
The boss owes **it to Sid**. (it = *direct object*)
The boss owes **him a month's salary**. (him = *indirect object*)
The boss owes **a month's salary to him**. (him = *indirect object*)

When both objects are pronouns, only one pattern is possible:
direct object + *to* / *for* + indirect object.
The boss owes **it to him**.
The boss ordered **it for him**.

1 Complete the sentences using the words in parentheses. Write each sentence in two different ways.

1. Finally, the waiter brought . . . (our dinners / us)
   Finally, the waiter brought us our dinners.
   Finally, the waiter brought our dinners to us.

2. After an hour of searching, the clerk gave . . . (a suitable pair of shoes / me)

3. At that café, they won't serve . . . (your meal / you) unless you pay for it in advance.

4. I didn't have any cash, so I handed . . . (my credit card / the clerk)

5. The potter at that shop promised . . . (a beautiful vase / my mother)

6. While they were swimming, their father ordered . . . (lunch / them)

7. I don't have any more cash, but I can pay . . . (the rest / you) tomorrow.

8. At the baseball game, the vendor threw . . . (a bag of peanuts / him)

2 Rewrite the following sentences in as many ways as possible using pronouns in place of the nouns in boldface.

1. The clerk gave **Maria the wrong blouse**.
   The clerk gave her the wrong blouse. / The clerk gave the wrong blouse to her. /
   The clerk gave it to Maria. / The clerk gave it to her.

2. The salesman sold **his last vacuum** to **John**.

3. That company still owes **Michael one week's pay**.

4. The real estate agent didn't mention **the leaky roof** to **the customers**.

5. The travel guide found **two wonderful antique shops** for **the tourists**.

6. Thomas reminded Daniel that he had promised **a diamond ring** to **Liz**.

7. The hotel chef made **my mother an omelet**.

8. After the receipt was printed, the clerk handed **Eleanor a pen**.

8B Verbs in the subjunctive

The following verbs can be followed by a *that* clause with a subjunctive verb.

advise   beg   require   stipulate
ask   prefer   specify   vote

He **advised that** his students **be** on time.
Our store policy clearly **stipulates that** all sales associates **report** to work by 8:30 A.M.

The negative subjunctive is formed with *not* and the base form of the verb.
The advertising executive's contract required that he **not receive** a bonus that year.

The passive form of the subjunctive is formed by *be* + past participle.
The sponsors asked that their product **be featured** prominently in the movie.
The manufacturers preferred that their shaving cream **not be endorsed** by misbehaving stars.

1 Complete the sentences using an active or passive subjunctive form of the verbs in the box. Verbs may be used more than once.

broadcast   not contain   give   prevent   remove   not send

1. The return policy stipulated that customers ___*be given*___ cash refunds for returned items.

2. A new guideline advises that telemarketers _____ from calling after 8:00 P.M.

3. It is required that an advertisement _____ any false information.

4. Parents begged that companies _____ from advertising candy on children's TV shows.

5. The contract clearly specifies that the station _____ our ads 24 hours a day.

6. The customer repeatedly asked that she _____ a free sample of the perfume.

7. I would prefer that companies _____ me spam e-mail of any kind.

8. We voted that those billboards blocking the town's ocean view _____.

2 Complete the sentences with an appropriate form of the verb in parentheses. Use the subjunctive when possible.

1. It's clear that the time devoted to commercials on TV _*has increased*_ (increase) over the past 10 years.

2. She advised that pressure _____ (apply) to companies that engage in false advertising.

3. I learned that my neighbor _____ (be) a stealth marketer.

4. The store required that each customer _____ (open) his or her bag for inspection.

5. He specified that this advertisement _____ (place) in this month's issue.

6. The actress begged that she _____ (not cast) in such a low-budget commercial.

7. I discovered that my sister _____ (be) addicted to shopping.

9A *Whenever* and *wherever* contrasted with *when* and *where*

If *whenever*, *wherever*, *when*, and *where* are followed by subject + *be* + adjective / past participle, the subject and *be* are often deleted. This occurs mainly in formal speech and writing.

Pet owners must take their pets to the vet **whenever / when** ~~taking them is~~ advisable.
Laws concerning the welfare of helper animals should be enforced **wherever / where** applicable.

Whenever and *wherever* can have the meaning "no matter when / where."
A: My dog doesn't like it when I give her a bath at night.
B: Mine doesn't like it **whenever** I give him a bath!

Whenever and *wherever* can also have the meaning "although I don't know when / where."
We'll have to get together on his birthday, **whenever** that is!
Their dog was found in a park outside of Hicksville, **wherever** that is!

Whenever and *wherever* are rarely used following the focus adverbs *even*, *just*, *right*, and *only*. *When* and *where* are often used instead.
My cats show me affection **even when** I'm in a bad mood.
Elephants will survive in the wild **only where** they are protected from illegal hunting.

---

1 Shorten the sentences by crossing out the subject and the form of *be* in the adverbial clause.

1. Pets need to be given attention every day, not just when ~~giving them attention is~~ convenient.

2. Dog owners are expected to use leashes to walk their dogs where using those items is required by law.

3. My veterinarian suggested that I buy Barkies brand dog food when Barkies brand is available.

4. Whenever disciplining them is appropriate, owners of intelligent animals must be prepared to discipline their pets.

5. Exotic animals may not be kept as pets wherever keeping such pets is prohibited by law.

2 Review the grammar rules on page 71. Complete the sentences with *when*, *whenever*, *where*, or *wherever*. Sometimes more than one answer is possible.

1. *When* _____ my dog ran out of the yard this morning, I called his name, but he kept on running.

2. _____ somebody walks past my house, my dog growls at him or her.

3. The insect looked so much like a leaf that I didn't notice it even _____ I looked right at it.

4. _____ we used to live, the landlord would let tenants have as many pets as they wanted.

5. The sign says that this parrot is from the Kakamega Forest, _____ that is!

6. Over the course of the year, _____ I visited her apartment, she seemed to have added another cat. By spring, she had at least five.

9B Noun clauses with *whoever* and *whatever*

In formal speech and writing, *whoever* is used for the subject and *whomever* is used for the object of a clause. *Whomever* is rare in conversation.

Whoever wants a unique experience should try scuba diving in a coral reef.

I'll take **whomever** the instructor chooses for my rock-climbing partner.

When referring to a known and limited group of items, *whichever* can be used to mean "whatever one" or "whatever ones."

For your birthday, I'll pay for kayaking or skydiving lessons. You can choose **whichever** you want.

I've packed three kinds of sandwiches for the picnic. Your friends can have **whichever** they want.

1 Complete the sentences with *whoever* or *whomever*.

1. I'm eating lunch outdoors today. ___*Whoever*___ wants to eat with me is welcome.

2. Access to this beach is strictly limited to residents and _____ they invite.

3. I believe urban environments without a significant presence of nature are unhealthy for _____ they surround.

4. _____ lives in that house must love the sun – it's made almost entirely of glass.

5. Some doctors say that spending more time in natural sunlight can be one source of relief for _____ winter depression afflicts.

6. _____ thinks that our city parks are just a waste of space has certainly lost touch with nature.

7. The manager position at the eco-resort will be filled by _____ the board of directors selects.

2 Fill in the blanks with *whoever*, *whatever*, or *whichever*.

Here's an idea for (1) ___*whoever*___ is feeling out of touch with nature. Why not enroll in a nature adventure program at a NaturVenture camp?

NaturVenture camps are convenient. Campers don't need to bring anything to our camps, because they can obtain (2) _____ they need from the camp stores. There's also a great selection of locations. There are four NaturVenture camps: on a river, in the forest, in the desert, and in the mountains.

In all four locations, we know how to get people in touch with nature! Our expert guides teach campers (3) _____ they want to know about kayaking, horseback riding, rock climbing, and many other outdoor activities. At our camps, we always keep safety in mind. Our trained medical staff is always on hand to assist (4) _____ might need help. The food is great, too. (5) _____ our chefs prepare always gets plenty of compliments.

Campers can choose (6) _____ of our four camps interests them. We offer one-week or two-week programs, so campers can choose (7) _____ suits their schedules and their budgets. And remember – there is a 10 percent discount for (8) _____ enrolls online. Sign up today!

The passive voice with a modal can be used in short answers.
A: Why wasn't that author awarded the Nobel Prize for literature?
B: I don't know, but he **should have been**. *(He should have been awarded the Nobel Prize for literature.)*

The verb *get* can also serve as an auxiliary to form the passive voice. It is less formal and primarily used in spoken English. *Get* always indicates a change (with a meaning close to *become*), while *be* can indicate an unchanging state or a dynamic one.
Larry and Natalie **got married** in 2006. *(Their wedding occurred in 2006.)*
Larry and Natalie **were married** in 2006 when they went to Greece. *(Their wedding may have occurred before 2006.)*

The verb *get* is also commonly used in expressions such as *get acquainted*, *get arrested*, *get dressed*, *get excited*, *get married*, and *get scared*.

1 Complete the short answers with the appropriate modal in the passive voice. Sometimes more than one answer is possible.

1. A: Will that Shakespeare class be offered next semester, too?
   B: Oh, yes. I'm absolutely sure that it _____*will be*_____.

2. A: Should text speak be used in essays by some students?
   B: Actually, I think it _____.

3. A: Could English be overtaken as the main international language someday?
   B: Well, in my opinion, it _____.

4. A: Was the television turned off when we went to bed?
   B: No, it wasn't, but it _____.

5. A: Would our class have been canceled if the teacher had been sick?
   B: Yes, it _____. Thank goodness she's not sick!

6. A: Do you think fluency in English can be achieved in five years?
   B: I'm pretty sure it _____, but you'd have to study and practice diligently.

2 Complete the sentences with the correct form of *be* or *get*.

1. While I was reading a book in the bathtub, I heard someone knocking, so I quickly _____*got*_____ dressed and answered the door.

2. Sam and Al had never met, so I gave them a few minutes to _____ acquainted.

3. Martin Luther King Jr. _____ remembered for his contribution to advancing civil rights for African Americans in the United States.

4. When she saw my father carrying her birthday gift, all of a sudden, my little sister _____ really excited and started jumping up and down.

5. I've never tried that language-learning method myself, but I know that it _____ designed by a famous professor.

10B Subject-verb agreement with quantifiers

A (*large / small / great*) *number of* always modifies a plural noun. The resulting expression takes a plural verb.
A (large) **number of students** in my English class **were** absent on Friday.

When certain collective nouns, such as *majority* or *minority*, act as a whole unit or a single group, they take a singular verb.
All students can express their opinions, but **the majority rules**.
In the United States, **Spanish speakers** constitute a linguistic **minority** that **is** growing rapidly.

Majority and *minority* are followed by the plural form of *be* when the complement is a plural noun.
If you ask my father about young people today, he'll tell you that **the majority are slackers**.
Of people who are concerned with using language correctly, only **a small minority are linguists**.

1 Review the rules for quantifiers on page 85. Choose the correct form of the verb. If both forms are possible, choose both.

1. A minority of American English speakers (understand)/(understands) Australian slang.

2. A great number of my friends *has / have* sharp tongues.

3. My students can't write without spell check. The majority *isn't / aren't* great spellers.

4. In the parliament, the newly elected majority *is / are* ready to make some changes.

5. A number of hip-hop expressions *has / have* been added to dictionaries.

6. A majority of my friends *has / have* a way with words.

7. There are times when a minority *speak / speaks* louder than a majority.

8. A number of languages *is / are* spoken in India.

2 Complete these sentences with the singular or plural simple present form of the verb in parentheses.

1. Each person _____*finds*_____ (find) the level of formality he or she is comfortable with.

2. No one _____ (know) the exact number of words in the English language.

3. Most of my friends _____ (speak) English fluently.

4. None of the linking verbs _____ (be) normally used in the passive voice.

5. A lot of people _____ (go) abroad to practice English.

6. A recent report indicated that about one-fourth of American high school students _____ (not graduate).

7. Plenty of my friends _____ (like) to send each other text messages.

8. Every language _____ (have) formal and less formal registers.

9. Every one of my in-laws _____ (talk) my ear off on the phone.

10. All fluent speakers _____ (need) to have an understanding of idiomatic language.

11A Compound adjectives

The following compound adjectives follow the pattern: noun + past participle.

awestruck	frostbitten	handwritten	homemade	store-bought	waterlogged
bloodstained	handmade	heartbroken	moth-eaten	sunburned	windswept

The following compound adjectives are found written as one word in many dictionaries.

airborne	barefooted	downhearted	lightweight	painstaking
airsick	daylong	hardheaded	newfound	seaworthy

In the comparative form of compound adjectives, *more* and *less* are not followed by hyphens.

a more forward-looking plan   a less easygoing person   a more highly trained applicant

1 Use one-word adjectives from the grammar box to rewrite the sentences.

1. The flight attendant helped the passengers who felt sick on the airplane.
   The flight attendant helped the airsick passengers.

2. We attended a meeting that lasted from 9:00 in the morning to 6:00 in the evening.

3. The passengers boarded the vessel that was worthy of making an ocean voyage.

4. The sailors stopped at an island that had only recently been discovered.

5. The star was overwhelmed by the fans who showed their admiration for her.

6. Jason caught a virus that was carried through the air.

2 Combine the words from both boxes to create compound adjectives and complete the sentences. Check a dictionary for meaning and hyphen use.

forward	hand	home	tender	broken	hearted	made	winded
frost	heart	long	widely	bitten	thinking	respected	written

1. The short __handwritten__ message on this photo of Marilyn Monroe makes it very valuable.

2. Because of his great experience in international affairs, the president is _____ in political circles.

3. The audience understood that they wouldn't be able to leave for a while; the speaker had a reputation for being _____.

4. Emma's boyfriend was exceptional. She was _____ when he moved away.

5. My grandmother would never serve anything store-bought. Her cakes and cookies were all _____.

6. Our country needs a more _____ leader, one who can prepare us for crises before they occur.

7. The _____ celebrity was well known for helping any needy person who contacted her.

8. The arctic explorers wore protective gear so that their hands and feet didn't get _____.

11B Superlative compound adjectives

The following adjectives and adverbs have irregular comparative and superlative forms. They are frequently used in comparative and superlative compound adjectives.

Adjective	Comparative	Superlative	Adverb	Comparative	Superlative
good	better	best	well	better	best
bad	worse	worst	badly	worse	worst
far	farther / further	farthest / furthest	little	less (lesser)	least
			much	more	most
			far	farther / further	farthest / furthest

As with other superlative adjectives, the article *the* is not used when the noun is preceded by a possessive.
Venezuela's **best-known** poet will be reading one of his works at the public library this week.

1 Write sentences as in the example using the information and the superlative form of the comparative adjective. Sometimes more than one answer is possible.

1. Charlize Theron is / good-looking actress / I've ever seen
   Charlize Theron is the best-looking actress I've ever seen.

2. My company president is / well-dressed executive / I've ever worked for

3. Last year, I went on one of / badly planned vacations / I've ever taken

4. Our chief of police is / little-appreciated public servant / our town has ever had

5. Mr. Fredericks is / well-loved teacher / our class has ever had

6. That player is / bad-tempered guy / our basketball team has ever hired

7. Professor Vargas is / much-honored academic / our college has ever invited to speak

8. That movie was filmed at / far-flung location / the studio has ever used

2 Write sentences using the superlative form of the compound adjective. Be careful to use hyphens and *the* correctly.

1. That company's (lightweight) camera is the Photoflash X25.
   That company's most lightweight camera is the Photoflash X25.
   That company's lightest-weight camera is the Photoflash X25.

2. My uncle's face looks (awestruck) in the photograph on the right.

3. Henry was (broad-minded) when it came to questions of cultural difference.

4. I take after my father, who is (hardheaded) man I know.

5. Joyce is quite smart, but she's not (well-read) person in the world.

6. To me, Japan's (awe-inspiring) sight is probably Mount Fuji.

7. Perhaps (widely recognized) actress from Malaysia is Michelle Yeoh.

8. One of the (low-lying) countries in Europe is Holland.

12A Subject-verb inversion in conditional sentences

When present or future real conditionals are expressed with *should* at the beginning of the sentence, the base form of the verb is used.
If you**'re** looking for a competent employee, Ted is your man.
Should you **be** looking for a competent employee, Ted is your man.

Subject-verb inversion in conditional sentences occurs rarely with *could* and *might*, usually in literary or archaic contexts, and often with adverbs such as *but* or *just*.
Could he **but** win her love, the world would be his.
Might I **just** see my country once more, my heart would find peace.

In formal situations, people sometimes replace *if* by putting the past subjunctive *were* at the beginning of unreal conditional sentences.
If she **found** enough investors, she could form a startup company.
Were she **to find** enough investors, she could form a startup company.

If she **had been** wealthy, she might not have gone into business.
Were she **to have been** wealthy, she might not have gone into business.

1 Rewrite these sentences using *should* at the beginning of the sentence and the base form of the verb.

1. If Sven goes into business for himself, I'm sure he'll do very well.
   Should Sven go into business for himself, I'm sure he'll do very well.

2. If Annie gets a raise, she'll be able to pay her college debts.

3. If Shin is sick tomorrow, would you be able to work in his place?

4. If you find yourself swamped by work, hire an assistant.

5. If a business is set up in a good location, customers will naturally come.

6. If a problem arises, you need to find a way to work around it.

7. If there's a chance of failure, I'd rather not take the risk.

8. If there's a lot of demand for a product, the price naturally rises.

2 Review the grammar rules on page 97 and in the grammar box. Then rewrite the sentences using subject-verb inversion.

1. If you asked him, he'd tell you the secret of his success.
   Were you to ask him, he'd tell you the secret of his success.

2. If the board approved the measure, the president would surely not veto it.

3. If his boss hadn't been working against him, Jake would have been promoted.

4. If I had looked at my calendar, I would have known about the meeting.

5. If I could just win the gold medal, I'd be happier than the richest man.

6. If we received adequate funding, our program could be a great success.

7. If they were aware of the risk, they would quickly patent their idea.

8. If Tamara hadn't spoken out, the boss would have ignored her.

12B Adverb clauses of condition

In the event (that) and *(just) in case* also introduce a condition on which another situation depends. *In the event (that)* is more formal.
In the event that a replacement cannot be found, you'll have to take on extra responsibilities.
Here's a number to call **just in case** the copy machine breaks down.

Whether or not is used instead of *if* to introduce a condition on which another situation depends. *Or not* is placed directly after *whether* or at the end of the clause.
Whether or not it involves travel, I'm going to have to take this job.
Whether it involves travel **or not**, I'm going to have to take this job.

Even if introduces a condition which, if it is true, doesn't affect the outcome of a situation. It is frequently used with *still*.
I'm (**still**) going to call in sick tomorrow **even if** I'm not actually sick.

If only introduces a condition that the speaker strongly wishes to be true.
If only I had known about that job opening, I would have applied for it immediately.

1 Match the clauses to make logical conditional sentences.

1. If only I hadn't insulted my boss, __e__

2. Whether you feel happy inside or not, ____

3. Even if you have great leadership skills, ____

4. Just in case you didn't get the memo, ____

5. If only I could wear casual clothes to work, ____

6. Whether or not the schedule is flexible, ____

7. Even if my company offers me a raise, ____

8. In the event that the manager retires, ____

a. here's a copy for your files.

b. I wouldn't have to spend so much money on suits.

c. you'll likely be promoted to fill her position.

d. I'm still going to take a job with another firm.

e. I'm sure he wouldn't have fired me.

f. the manager wants you to smile for the customers.

g. you can't be forced to work more than 40 hours a week.

h. you still have to earn the workers' respect.

2 Choose the expression that best completes the sentence.

1. *Just in case* / *If only* I have to go on a business trip this week, I've kept my schedule open.

2. *Even if* / *Assuming that* the weather is nice, this weekend's company picnic should be fun.

3. *In the event that* / *Whether or not* I receive training, I'm still not confident in my abilities.

4. *Even if* / *If only* I were in charge of hiring people, I'd give everybody a pay raise.

5. *Provided that* / *Just in case* employees do what is required, salaries are increased every year.

VOCABULARY PLUS

7A Prefixes to create antonyms

Cross out the word that does <u>not</u> fit the meaning of each sentence.

1. A: Today I saw a driver in a car at a stoplight. He was texting, talking on a cell phone, and had his laptop open – all at once!

   B: Unfortunately, that seems to be a common practice these days. It seems *indecisive* / *illogical* / *irresponsible* to me.

2. A: My sister really surprised me the other day. She actually picked up her clothes from the floor and cleaned our room!

   B: I used to think she was pretty *irresponsible* / *immature* / *intolerant*, but I guess she's changing.

3. A: My nephew hasn't even tried to get a job since he graduated. He lives with his parents, doesn't pay rent, and stays out all night.

   B: Wow, he sounds like an *inconsiderate* / *immature* / *inconsistent* person. It must be hard on your aunt and uncle. Maybe he'd be motivated if they made him pay rent.

4. A: A recent article said that it's becoming common for people to be expected to work extremely long hours in some professions.

   B: Yes, I've heard that lawyers often work past midnight to prepare for big trials. It's considered *indecisive* / *irresponsible* / *improper* to leave the office before being completely prepared.

7B Collocations with *change*

Correct the underlined mistake in each sentence. Write the correct form of a word or phrase from the box.

anticipate	bring about	cope with	go through	welcome

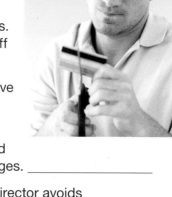

1. Some people get into financial trouble because they use their credit cards all the time and are unable to make their payments. Then they have to <u>anticipate</u> serious lifestyle changes to pay off their debt. ____*go through*____

2. The mayor is admired for consistently initiating action to improve the city. He is always looking for ways to <u>cope with</u> change.

   _____

3. A few longtime residents want everything in their neighborhood to stay the same. They're not the type of people to <u>resist</u> changes. _____

4. The company plans to provide more on-the-job training. The director <u>avoids</u> this change will lead to a more knowledgeable and productive staff. _____

5. During the last recession, some people were unemployed for several months. They <u>welcomed</u> some difficult changes by relying on their families for support.

8A Expressions to discuss shopping

Use the correct form of the expressions from the box to complete the text.

make an impulse buy	be a compulsive shopper	go over her credit limit
go window-shopping	have buyer's remorse	be a bargain hunter

Did you ever notice how people have different shopping styles? My mom has always been price conscious and (1) ___*is a bargain hunter*___. Whenever there's a sale, she combs through everything, looking for the lowest prices. On the other hand, my friend Maggie doesn't even look at price tags and buys everything in sight. She just can't control her urge to shop. She definitely (2) _____. She often spends more than the bank allows on her charge cards, but doesn't worry about (3) _____. Now, my sister Shelly has a totally different shopping style. She drives me insane because she never buys anything. She prefers to (4) _____, just peering at the displays of the latest fashions. Crazy, right? As for me, I have to admit that at times, I have the urge to go on a shopping spree. Shopping is all about having fun. I certainly don't plan to buy three pairs of shoes, but all of a sudden, there they are in my shopping bag! OK, I admit to (5) _____ every once in a while. But I confess that I (6) _____ on occasion and end up returning things. There's only so much room in my closets!

8B Marketing strategies

Read the situations. Then choose the correct ending to make a true sentence.

1. That actress made a commercial for a new floral perfume. She makes a point of saying that she wears it in real life. The perfume maker . . .

   ☐ a. is offering a comparative-marketing program.
   ☐ b. must think a celebrity endorsement will increase sales.

2. Every time the main character on that sitcom has breakfast, viewers can clearly see the product name on the box of cereal on the table. That cereal company . . .

   ☐ a. is using a product-placement strategy.
   ☐ b. is offering free samples.

3. The credit card company gives points every time shoppers use their card. Many customers keep the card for a long time to earn points. The credit card company retains its customers by using . . .

   ☐ a. a loyalty program.
   ☐ b. coupon codes.

4. When consumers searched for smartphone features and prices, one brand kept popping up. As part of its marketing strategy, the smartphone company is using . . .

   ☐ a. word-of-mouth marketing.
   ☐ b. search-engine marketing.

9A Physical features of animals

Choose the correct words to complete the conversation.

Ahn: I've been studying how animals defend themselves. It's fascinating how a bird can use its (1) *feathers / fangs /* (beak) to fight off predators.

Phil: Birds can be fierce, especially if they're protecting their nests.

Ahn: Speaking of fierce, when I was hiking last week, I ran across a herd of wild mountain goats. Two male goats were in a battle, using their (2) *horns / scales / gills* and (3) *claws / hooves / tusks*.

Phil: Goats are considered to be smart, and they are amazing climbers. What other animals have you studied?

Ahn: Last year, I spent time at an ocean research facility to study dolphins.

Phil: Oh, my eight-year-old son has been fascinated by them lately. Someone told him that dolphins didn't have (4) *fins / scales / tails* and didn't breathe through (5) *gills / paws / wings*, and he was really puzzled – "Why not, if they live in the ocean?" When I explained that dolphins are mammals, and not fish, he was amazed. Now he reads every dolphin book he can find.

Ahn: Hey, maybe he'll want to study animals someday, like I do!

9B Nature-related idioms

Replace the underlined phrases with the correct idioms from the list.

| a breath of fresh air | as clear as mud | set in stone | under the weather |
| a drop in the ocean | a walk in the park | the tip of the iceberg | up in the air |

1. They're going to open the new nature preserve to the public sometime soon, though the exact date is still <u>not decided on</u>. ___*up in the air*___

2. I know my own effort to reduce carbon pollution by driving an electric car is just <u>a small thing</u>, but I like to know I'm doing something to help. _____

3. I've been feeling <u>unwell</u> for days now. I should really see my doctor. _____

4. A politician helping clean up the park is <u>something new and exciting</u>! I wish more public officials would help the community. _____

5. His explanation of the new environmental law was <u>extremely confusing</u>. I still have no idea of what it's about! _____

6. People are cutting down trees illegally, but I'm sure that's just <u>a small part of the problem</u>. There are bound to be more problems than that. _____

7. I was nervous about presenting my research to the Conservation Board, but in the end it was <u>really easy</u>. They were such good listeners! _____

8. The timetable for the conference is <u>unchangeable</u>. There's no way we can reschedule.

   _____

10A Discourse markers

Cross out the discourse marker that does not fit the meaning of the sentence.

Greetings, jobseekers!

Do job interviews make you nervous? I used to feel that way, too, but not anymore. My advice is to be prepared for the interview. (1) *Furthermore* / *To begin* / *First of all*, do some research on the company you will interview with, so you can talk about the company in an informed way during the interview. Learn about its business goals, products and services, and financial health. (2) *Next* / *Nevertheless* / *Second*, anticipate the questions the interviewer may ask you – and think of good answers! (3) *Yet* / *In addition* / *Furthermore*, it's a good idea to jot down your own questions about job responsibilities and opportunities for growth. At this point, you may feel totally ready for your interview. (4) *Likewise* / *Yet* / *Nevertheless*, there's one more step you should take: role-play an interview with a trusted friend or relative. That will increase your ability to communicate with self-assurance. (5) *In conclusion* / *To sum up* / *Similarly*, it may feel like all this preparation is a lot of work, but it'll be worth it when you walk confidently into that interview room.

10B Idioms related to the use of language

Complete the sentence about each situation using an expression from the box.
Use the correct form of the verbs and pronouns.

have a sharp tongue	stick to the point	talk behind someone's back
have a way with words	talk around a point	talk someone's ear off

1. Last night, Jessica called Mei Ling and discussed her personal problems for three hours. Mei Ling didn't know how to get her friend off the phone!

   Mei Ling thought that Jessica was *talking her ear off* .

2. Tom began his presentation by talking about oil drilling in Alaska. Then suddenly, he changed the subject to farming methods in China. The audience seemed a little confused.

   Tom needed to _____ .

3. My uncle often criticizes my cousin about his grades, his choice of friends, and how little he helps around the house. I think sometimes my uncle is a little harsh.

   My uncle can sometimes _____ .

4. Ron is one of those salespeople who can talk his customers into buying anything! I once saw him convince a guy to spend half his salary on a ring for his girlfriend.

   Ron certainly _____ .

5. When Pat has to discuss a thorny issue with a friend, she never addresses the problem directly. People get frustrated because she won't say what's really bothering her.

   Pat has to stop _____ .

6. After we left the party, Josh started complaining about how unfriendly Anna was. I told him that it was unfair to talk about someone who wasn't there to defend herself.

   I wanted Josh to stop _____ .

Choose the true statement for each sentence.

1. To be effective during a crisis, it's a good idea not to get overly emotional.
   - ☐ a. You should remain coolheaded even during a crisis.
   - ☐ b. You should be cold-hearted even during a crisis.

2. People should be willing to consider different points of view, no matter how extreme.
   - ☐ a. People should be absent-minded about different points of view.
   - ☐ b. People should be open-minded about different points of view.

3. Some people can be stubborn about doing things their own way and rarely compromise.
   - ☐ a. People who can't make compromises are hard-hearted and poor team players.
   - ☐ b. People who can't make compromises are hard-headed and poor team players.

4. Mammals maintain a fairly constant body temperature, regardless of their environment.
   - ☐ a. Mammals are warm-blooded creatures.
   - ☐ b. Mammals are warm-hearted creatures.

5. Some folks have little tolerance for people who have different beliefs or ideas.
   - ☐ a. It's unfortunate that some folks are so empty-headed about others.
   - ☐ b. It's unfortunate that some folks are so narrow-minded about others.

11B Phrasal verbs

Choose the correct words to complete the conversation.

Amy: I have to fly home this weekend to (1) *take after* / (check on) my grandparents. They don't like to admit it, but they can use a little help around the house these days.

Luke: You go home a lot, don't you? That's great that you (2) *look after* / *look to* your grandparents!

Amy: Well, I feel compelled to (3) *get through* / *live up to* my responsibilities. Besides, my grandparents took such good care of me as a child. Now it's my turn!

Luke: It sounds like you (4) *take after* / *side with* your grandparents! They must be excellent role models for you and your brothers.

Amy: Unfortunately, my younger brother Ethan is having a hard time at school. I'm going to talk with him this weekend. He needs to (5) *face up to* / *live up to* his problems. I think I'll remind him about the challenges our grandparents faced when they were young, and how they were still able to finish college.

Luke: I'm sure that you'll help him (6) *get through* / *look to* this difficult period.

12A Prepositions following *work*

Complete the conversations with the words from the box. Use the correct form of the verbs.

work against   work around   work for   work off   work toward

1. A: We've been discussing this issue with the manufacturer for months. The engineers are getting close to figuring out a way to make the batteries last longer.

   B: That's great! Sounds like you're ___*working toward*___ a solution.

2. A: We don't have enough staff to finish the analysis on time. We've asked management for help, but they can't hire any new people right now.

   B: That's too bad! It seems like your bosses are _____ you.

3. A: My parents lent me a lot of money, and I don't know how to pay them back.

   B: Do they need help around their house? Maybe you could _____ some of your debt by doing yard work, cleaning the garage, and things like that.

4. A: Our firm has offices in Beijing and New York. Sometimes it's tricky to juggle the time zones, especially when we're trying to schedule meetings.

   B: Having colleagues in different locations can be a challenge, but hopefully you'll find a way to _____ that problem.

5. A: My last boss was extremely demanding. I learned a lot from her, but it was tough working 80 hours a week! If she was in the office, we had to be there, too.

   B: Sounds like a valuable learning experience. In the future, I hope you get to _____ a manager with a more balanced approach to life!

12B Expressions related to success in the workplace

Choose the best words to complete the email.

Hello Mark,

Thank you for agreeing to write the job description for our new position. Here are my thoughts on what to include when you write it. Since this is an entrepreneurial company, we should put a high priority on finding someone who has original ideas and (1) *is innovative* / *has charisma* / *has influence*. We need a person who (2) *has specialized training* / *has initiative* / *has influence* and doesn't wait to be told what to do. In addition, since our company works in close-knit teams, the new hire should (3) *have good communication skills* / *have self-discipline* / *be optimistic* and be good at explaining ideas. We also want a candidate who (4) *has specialized training* / *is conscientious* / *has leadership ability* and can inspire others to do their best work. Finally, since we deal with a lot of internal and external change, the person we hire must (5) *be adaptable* / *be trustworthy* / *be conscientious* and able to cope with some degree of uncertainty.

I look forward to reading the job description.

Regards,

Laura

Credits

Illustration credits

Jo Goodberry: 12, 103
Paul Hostetler: 22, 23, 64, 101

Kim Johnson: 3, 26, 36, 65
Dan McGeehan: 41, 56, 84

Rob Schuster: 72, 87
Koren Shadmi: 9, 17, 53, 83

James Yamasaki: 28, 86

Photography credits

Back cover: (*clockwise from top center*) ©Leszek Bogdewicz/Shutterstock, ©Wavebreak Media/Thinkstock, ©Blend Images/Alamy, ©limpido/Shutterstock; 2 ©George Doyle/Thinkstock; 5 ©Davide Mazzoran/Thinkstock; 6 (*left to right*) ©Corbis/SupersStock, ©Jeff Greenberg/Alamy, ©Blend Images/Alamy; 8 ©Corbis/SuperStock; 10 (*top to bottom*) ©Coprid/Shutterstock, ©Neamov/Shutterstock, ©Barghest/Shutterstock, ©robert_s/Shutterstock, ©mama_mia/Shutterstock; 11 ©Ira Berger/Alamy; 13 ©alexnika/Thinkstock; 14 ©Fuse/Thinkstock; 15 ©Cultura Limited/SuperStock; 16 (*clockwise from top left*) ©Dimitrios Kambouris/Getty Images, ©Alberto E. Rodriguez/Getty Images, ©Jeffrey Mayer/WireImage/Getty Images, ©Vittorio Zunino Celotto/Getty Images; 18 (*left to right*) ©Krzysztof Gawor/Getty Images, ©Science Photo Library – SCIEPRO/Getty Images, ©Eric Isselée/Thinkstock; 19 ©EVERETT KENNEDY BROWN/epa/Corbis; 20 ©Beyond/SuperStock; 21 ©Gilles Podevins/Science Photo Library/Corbis; 24 ©Europics/Newscom; 25 ©Newspix/Getty Images; 27 (*clockwise from top left*) ©Christin Gilbert/agefotostock/SuperStock, ©al_ter/Thinkstock, ©Franck Boston/Thinkstock, ©GregC/Thinkstock, ©Nathan Allred/Thinkstock, ©Comstock/Thinkstock; 29 ©Photimageon/Alamy; 31 (*top to bottom*) ©Stockbyte/Thinkstock, ©Mykola Velychko/Thinkstock, ©Jupiterimages/Thinkstock, ©Valeriy Lebedev/Thinkstock; 32 (*clockwise from top left*) ©Jupiterimages/Thinkstock, ©Maksim Kabakou/Thinkstock, ©Elnur Amikishiyev/Thinkstock, ©Paul Poplis/Getty Images, ©guy harrop/Alamy; 33 ©Eric Staller/Splash News/Newscom; 34 ©GERARD CERLES/Getty Images; 35 ©MANAN VATSYAYANA/Getty Images; 38 ©I love images/SuperStock; 39 ©AF archive/Alamy; 42 ©Digital Vision/Thinkstock; 43 (*top to bottom*) ©courtesy of One Day on Earth, ©courtesy of One Day on Earth, ©courtesy of One Day on Earth; 44 ©OJO Images/SuperStock; 45 ©RichardBaker/Alamy; 46 ©Fernando Garcia-Murga/AgeFotostock; 47 (*left to right*) ©Fox Photos/Getty Images, ©Dave J Hogan/Getty Images; 48 (*left to right*) ©Kevin Winter/Getty Images, ©John Shearer/Getty Images, ©Chris McGrath/Getty Images; 49 ©Stanislav Tiplyashin/Thinkstock; 50 ©Jack Hollingsworth/Thinkstock; 51 ©Red Box Films/ZUMA Press/Newscom; 52 ©CBS/Getty Images; 54 ©Exactostock/SuperStock; 57 ©Wavebreakmedia Ltd/Thinkstock; 58 (*left to right*) ©Jose Luis Pelaez Inc/Blend Images/Alamy, ©Image Source/Alamy, ©David Litschel/Alamy; 59 ©Sergey Mikhailov/Thinkstock; 62 (*clockwise from top left*) ©Iryna Rasko/Shutterstock, ©Nastco/Thinkstock, ©Jupiterimages/Thinkstock, ©Ilya Shapovalov/Shutterstock; 63 ©james turner/Alamy; 66 (*left to right*) ©Art Directors & TRIP/Alamy, ©Raine Vara/Alamy, ©Raymond Boyd/Getty Images; 67 ©John Wynn/Thinkstock; 69 ©Photos 12/Alamy; 70 (*clockwise from top left*) ©Presselect/Alamy, ©Jean-Louis Atlan/Corbis, ©Rick Friedman/Corbis, ©Paris Match/Getty Images; 71 ©Photo by Adam Scull/Newscom; 73 ©Image Source/Getty Images; 74 ©Brad Perks Lightscapes/Alamy; 75 ©Getty Images/Agefotostock; 76 ©David De Lossy/Thinkstock; 77 ©STAN HONDA/Getty Images; 78 (*left to right*) ©Purestock/Thinkstock, ©Flirt/SuperStock, ©iStock/Thinkstock; 79 (*left to right*) ©iStock Collection/Thinkstock, ©Mitchell Kranz/Shutterstock, ©Fuse/Thinkstock; 80 (*left to right*) ©Tim Mosenfelder/Getty Image News/Getty Images, ©AFP/Getty Images; 82 ©Khakimullin Aleksandr/Shutterstock; 85 ©Tom Briglia/Getty Images; 88 (*left to right*) ©Elliot & Fry/Getty Images, ©Nick Harvey/WireImage/Getty Images, ©Michael Tran/FilmMagic/Getty Images; 90 (*clockwise from top left*) ©Christian Alminana/WireImage/Getty Images, ©L. Busacca/WireImage/Getty Images, ©Valerie Macon/Getty Images, ©Michael Kovac/WireImage/Getty Images, ©John Parra/WireImage/Getty Images; 91 ©Ian Gavan/Getty Images; 92 (*top to bottom*) ©iStock Collection/Thinkstock, ©iStock Collection/Thinkstock, ©iStock Collection/Thinkstock, ©Blend Images/Shutterstock, ©Siri Stafford/Thinkstock, ©gulfimages/SuperStock; 93 ©Jacek Sopotnicki/Thinkstock; 94 ©itanistock/Alamy; 95 ©VMAA/ZOB WENN Photos/Newscom; 96 (*clockwise from top right*) ©Bryan Smith/ZUMAPRESS/Newscom, ©YOSHIKAZU TSUNO/AFP/Getty Images/Newscom, ©Andrew Hasson/Photoshot/Getty Images; 100 ©Comstock Images/Thinkstock; 102 ©mediaphotos/Thinkstock; 105 (*left to right*) ©Jacob Wackerhausen/Thinkstock, ©Suprijono Suharjoto/Thinkstock, ©Chace & Smith Photography/Fuse Collection/Thinkstock; 131 ©mangostock/Thinkstock; 133 ©Mark A Schneider/Getty Images; 135 ©Blend Images/SuperStock; 136 ©George Doyle/Thinkstock; 138 ©William Curch – Summit42.com/Getty Images; 140 ©Agefotostock/SuperStock

Text credits

The authors and publishers acknowledge the following sources of copyright material and are grateful for the permissions granted. While every effort has been made, it has not always been possible to identify the sources of all the material used, or to trace all copyright holders. If any omissions are brought to our notice, we will be happy to include the appropriate acknowledgments on reprinting.

9 Adapted from "How Social Media 'Friends' Translate Into Real-Life Friendships" by Terri Thornton, *Mediashift*, July 13, 2011. Reproduced with permission of Mediashift, PBS; 16 Adapted from "Judging Faces Comes Naturally" by Jules Crittenden, *Boston Herald*, September 7, 1997. Reproduced with permission of the Boston Herald; 17 Adapted from "Overcoming a Bad First Impression" by Susan Fee, Professional Clinical Counselor, www.susanfee.com. Reproduced with permission of Susan Fee; 25 Adapted from "Family: I Unplugged My Kids" by Melissa McClements, *The Guardian*, January 1, 2011. Copyright © Guardian News & Media Ltd 2011; 35 Adapted from "Do Good-luck Charms Really Work in Competitions?" by Alex Hutchinson, *The Globe and Mail*, October 18, 2010. Reproduced with permission of Alex Hutchinson; 43 Adapted from "'One Day On Earth' Debuts Worldwide, Offers Time Capsule Of Our Lives" by Mark Johanson, *International Business Times*, April 21, 2012. Reproduced with permission of International Business Times; 51 Adapted from "Sixto Rodriguez: On the Trail of the Dylan of Detroit" by David Gritten, *The Telegraph*, June 14, 2012. Copyright © Telegraph Media Group Limited 2012; 61 Adapted from "Living the Simple Life – and Loving It" by Julia Duin, *The Washington Times*, January 5, 1996. Copyright © 1996 The Washington Times LLC. This reprint does not constitute or imply any endorsement or sponsorship of any product, service, company or organization. License # 37237; 69 Adapted from "Word-of-Mouth Marketing: We All Want to Keep Up with the Joneses" by Martin Lindstrom, www.martinlindstrom.com, September 21, 2011. Reproduced with permission of Martin Lindstrom; 77 From "A Summer Job That Promises Nature Walks for Pay" by Cara Buckley, *The New York Times*, August 13, 2008. Copyright © 2008 The New York Times. All rights reserved. Used by permission and protected by the Copyright Laws of the United States. The printing, copying, redistribution, or retransmission of this Content without express written permission is prohibited; 80 Adapted from *Schaum's Quick Guide to Great Presentation Skills* by Melody Templeton and Suzanne Sparks Fitzgerald, published by McGraw-Hill, 1999. Copyright © 1999 by the McGraw-Hill Companies, Inc.; 87 Adapted from "Slang Abroad" by Ben Falk, *The Daily Colonial*, April 1, 2006. Reproduced with permission; 95 Adapted from "Leading Questions" by Alison Benjamin, *The Guardian*, March 28, 2007. Copyright © Guardian News & Media Ltd 2007; 103 Adapted from *Job Savvy: How to Be a Success at Work Fifth Edition* by LaVerne L. Ludden, published by JIST Publishing, 2012. Reproduced with permission of JIST Publishing.

Answers

Page 32, Exercise 1B: Story 2 is false.
Page 34, Exercise 5B: They are all hoaxes.
Page 84, Exercise 2A: before, Are you OK?, See you later, excellent, great, tonight